Escaping the D in the Three Realms:

Relationships, Thinking and Dreaming

Joseph Dillard

*Dedicated to the piercing of samsara and
the overcoming of dukkha, suffering.*

Copyright © 2017 Joseph Dillard
Integral Deep Listening Press, Berlin
All rights reserved.
ISBN-13: 978-1544254883
ISBN-10: 1544254881

Also by Joseph Dillard

Dreamworking:
How to Use Your Dreams for Creative Problem Solving
Transformational Dreamwork:
Toward an Integral Approach to Deep Listening
Waking Up
Integral Deep Listening Interviewing Techniques
Integral Deep Listening Practitioner
Integral Deep Listening and Healing
Integral Deep Listening and Meditation
Dream Sociometry
The Dream Sociomatrix
Integral Deep Listening: Awakening Your Life compass
Transcending Your Monkey Mind:
The Five Trees and Meditation
Ending Nightmares for Good
Integral Deep Listening Case Studies
Light from Heaven: Deep Listening to Near Death Experiences.
Words and Concepts that Are and Are Not Conducive to Enlightenment:
Understanding Principles Fundamental to Integral Deep Listening
Seven Octaves of Enlightenment: Integral Deep Listening Pranayama
Dream Yoga: Der weg der Träume

Preface

Escaping the Drama Triangle in the Three Realms: Relationships, Thinking and Dreaming is a rewriting and compilation of essays on the Drama Triangle that have appeared at IntegralDeepListening.com, DreamYoga.com over the years. Consequently, the reader will find quite a bit of redundancy. While this could have been removed, these concepts are important enough to bear repeating in different contexts and in different ways so that they are heard again and again until they are understood, learned and applied.

The good news is that none of us have to stay stuck in the Drama Triangle, at least not in the varieties that routinely haunt us today. There are a number of powerful tools to get unstuck that are discussed here, including understanding the concepts and how they show up in life, identifying the associated words and cognitive distortions that perpetuate identification with this or that role and learning to access emerging potentials that are much less stuck in drama and therefore have potentially unique recommendations that are tailor-made to move us into greater clarity, freedom, inner peace and wakefulness.

Because the Drama Triangle is no respecter of culture, age, religion or intelligence the only protection you and your loved ones have is the extent to which you extract yourself from it and create relationships that recognize and call it out when it appears, while you assertively work to neutralize it. This is a lifelong pursuit, but one that is highly rewarding in many ways, including the expanding quality of a simplified life. This may seem like a trivial asset, but it is fundamental to happiness, no matter who you are, where you live, when you live or what you do with your time.

As with all of Integral Deep Listening (IDL), claims made about what the Drama Triangle is and how to get out of it are not to be believed or taken on faith but rather tested in your own life. This book is meant to be practical, to move you into action so that you will test its premises and, in the process, create a life that more fully reflects the priorities of life itself, awakening in and through you.

February 14, 2017
Berlin

Table of Contents

1: How You Keep Yourself Stuck in Drama and How to Get Out 1
2: Freeing Yourself from the Drama Triangle..........................13
3: The Drama Triangle in the Three Realms: 19
4: The Drama Triangle as a 28
5: How the Drama Triangle Shows Up in The Three Realms..............31
6: Love and the Drama Triangle.....................................45
7. Addiction and the Drama Triangle
8: Getting Out of the Drama Triangle...............................55
9: Using the Empowerment Dynamic..................................59
10: Ways Feelings Keep You Stuck in Drama..........................62
11: Words that Keep You Stuck in Drama.............................70
12: Conscience and the Drama Triangle..............................79
13: How Our World View Keeps Us Stuck in the Drama Triangle.........90
14: How the Drama Triangle in Your Dreams Affects Your Health.......121
15: Medicine and the Drama Triangle................................130
16: The Wizard of Oz and the Merging of Waking and Night Time Dreams in the Drama Triangle......................................140
17: Healing Social Nightmares......................................143
18: The Drama Triangle and Economic Sanity.........................145
19: Terrorism and the Drama Triangle...............................148
20: Global Warming and the Drama Triangle..........................150
21: Meditation and the Drama Triangle..............................152
22: Lucid Dreaming and the Drama Triangle..........................162
23: Near Death Experiences and the Drama Triangle..................168

1: How You Keep Yourself Stuck in Drama and How to Get Out

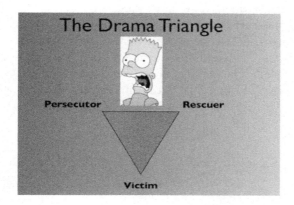

The Drama Triangle in the Three Realms

    First described by Stephen Karpman in a 1968 essay, the Drama Triangle consists of three roles, Persecutor, Victim and Rescuer. A protagonist or hero rescues someone who is being persecuted by some evil person or power, and that rescued person is, therefore, a Victim. In the process, the Rescuer becomes the Victim of the powers of the Persecutor as well, but in the end, the Persecutor becomes the Victim of the Re2222scuer's superior abilities.

    If this sounds familiar, it is because this is the plot of almost every cartoon and drama that you have ever read or seen. It also can be observed in almost every major historical event in the history of the world, from the life of Buddha, the life and death of Jesus, Julius Caesar, the rise of Islam, the Inquisition, the colonization of the West, Abraham Lincoln's battles with Congress, the Armenian holocaust, the Apollo program, and the economic meltdown of 2008. And that's not all. If you stop and examine them, your thoughts and feelings are immersed in the Drama Triangle. Every night, you dream this plot; if you take a look at your dream journal you will generally find yourself in the role of victim of some threatening or confusing persecuting individual, object, and situation. If a Rescuer does not appear, you may rescue yourself by attacking the Persecutor, switching to a different dream ("changing the channel!") or waking yourself up. The Drama Triangle is probably a major component of your nightly dreams, whether you remember them or not. Relationships, thoughts and dreams are the three realms where the Drama Triangle can defeat your happiness and undercut your peace of mind.

    Drama can be educational, entertaining and valuable, but being the victim of drama means living your life on an emotional roller-coaster without any peace of mind or understanding of why things turn out painfully for you despite your best intentions. When you're in the Drama Triangle, life is always intense but things never change. You're stuck. You stay stuck. You get used to being miserable. Drama becomes natural after months and years of adaptation. When you can't imagine a meaningful life without it, you are probably addicted to drama. Some common indications of an addiction to drama include taking things personally, worrying about what others think about you, worrying about the future, guilt about the past, fear of failure, fear of rejection, yelling and poor impulse control, and nightmares. Here are descriptions of the three roles.

The Role of Persecutor

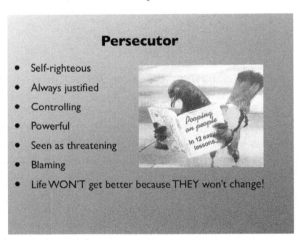

Persecutor
- Self-righteous
- Always justified
- Controlling
- Powerful
- Seen as threatening
- Blaming
- Life WON'T get better because THEY won't change!

We rarely see ourselves as Persecutors. Parents say, "I am only punishing you for your own good." When is such a statement educational and when is it abusive? Bosses say, "I don't want to fire you; it's nothing personal." When is such a statement "creative destruction," (a capitalist term for justifying firing people), and when is it worker exploitation? Soldiers think, "I am only killing the enemy because they are aggressors and I'm making the world safe." Is killing ever justified or is it always persecution? Grand Inquisitors say, "I am only torturing you to save your soul." When is warfare and cruelty just and when is it simply persecution in the Drama Triangle? How can you tell the difference with any certainty? These questions are important, because when you get into the role of the Persecutor, you're reinforcing both selfishness and inhumanity. These are all examples of playing the role of Persecutor in the first domain, the realm of your interpersonal relationships. We will talk about self-persecution in your thoughts and night time dreams below.

1: How You Keep Yourself Stuck in Drama and How to Get Out

The first and most fundamental characteristic of the Persecutor role is self-righteousness. Persecutors know what is best, not only for themselves, but for others. Persecutorial actions are justified in their eyes and, therefore, are never abusive. You can see how law enforcement agents, from the President to judges to police, routinely fail to distinguish between the common good and persecution, in order to justify short-term goals that improve their reputation or career status, get them re-elected, reappointed, or make them money.

When you are in the role of persecutor, people are getting what they deserve, or you are only doing what you have to do. Perhaps you justify it because the other person broke rules, is a threat to the nation, or because it is "God's will." Persecutors often frame themselves as Victims. They will say, "This hurts me worse than it does you." They may see themselves as having no choice, themselves the victim of unfair laws, work policies they must follow, or the directives of their military commander, employer, government or God. Monarchs, dictators, presidents, and prime ministers justify persecution by saying they have no choice. They must limit personal freedoms of citizens to ensure national security; they must wage war because it is their duty. It's nothing personal.

What's going on here? Persecutors seek control and fear being out of control. They think that if they can just get enough power, then not only will their life go smoothly, but yours will, too. Like a good parent, they say, "Trust me. I know what's best for you. You must obey me, for your own good. If you do not, I will punish you, but only because I care so much for you." If this sounds twisted, grotesque, cruel, wrong, yet all too familiar, it is because occupying the role of the Persecutor is all of these things.

When things don't work out, Persecutors blame others. Parents tend to blame the schools for the failures of their children. Politicians blame the opposition for their own lack of leadership. Lawyers, judges and police blame bad laws or "the system" for their own arbitrariness and cruelty. This is called "changing the subject." You hope to divert responsibility from yourself to others. The price that you pay is that you give your power away to whatever or whomever you see as the source of your unhappiness. Your hands are tied because of God, the government, the rules of the department, or the need for "discipline." If that doesn't work, you may tell yourself that others don't understand; you didn't mean to be hurtful, cruel or unfair; or you were only trying to help. You may even say, "It was only a joke! Can't you take a joke?" If none of this works, and often even when it does, you may persecute yourself by falling into guilt. Then, you may do things to punish yourself: tell yourself that you were wrong or stupid, that you are a failure; feel angry at yourself for your actions; attempt to lose yourself in alcohol, drugs or other mindless, unrelated forms of escapism. This is an example of the role of Persecutor in the second domain, of your thoughts and feelings.

When you persecute others, you may be trying to avoid what feels like self-persecution by putting the responsibility elsewhere. When you think your choice is to either blame others or blame yourself, it's easy to see how and why you choose to blame others. However, when you persecute others, you are persecuting the parts of yourself that they represent. Consequently, *persecution of others is always self-persecution.* Self-persecution is the core problem that leads to the blaming of others. If you learn to stop blaming yourself, you will stop blaming others. However, the inverse is not true: if you stop blaming others you are unlikely to therefore stop blaming yourself. Therefore, Integral Deep Listening (IDL) focuses on stopping the Drama Triangle by teaching you that self-blame is *never* helpful or productive and by showing you how to stop blaming yourself.

It is important to recognize that guilt is self-persecution. If this is true, then when you choose to use guilt to make children behave or get your partner to change their behavior, then you are persecuting the parts of yourself that they represent, in addition to immersing your relationship even deeper into the dream or delusional reality of the Drama Triangle. When you feel guilty, you are not only persecuting yourself, you are condemning yourself to life inside the Drama Triangle. If you want to get out, you have to realize you have an addiction to guilt that you have to break. One way of doing so is to stop using the language of guilt in your speech and thoughts. This means to ask others to catch you using the words "should," "ought," and "must." It means learning to stop using these words. It means to learn to substitute other words, such as "want to" or "prefer to," not only in your speech but in your thoughts. This strategy will be explained in more detail below, in the chapter on words that keep you stuck in drama.

Life never gets better for Persecutors because the world won't change to conform to their unrealistic expectations. However, that doesn't keep them from continuing to believe that it *should*. Therefore, they continue their futile attempts to make others responsible for both their happiness and their pain, and to blame others or themselves when the world doesn't act the way they think it should. While Persecutors often don't see themselves as threatening, they use intimidation and threats to get what they want.

The third way that you stay stuck in the persecutor role in the Drama Triangle is in your night time dreams, whether you remember them or not. You do this in several ways. When you see a dream threat, such as a monster or a fire, isn't that some aspect of yourself you are reacting to? If that is so, aren't you scaring yourself? If that is so, aren't you persecuting yourself within the Drama Triangle?

A second type of dream persecution is when you attack, abuse, or ignore another character in a dream. Is that not persecution? If so, who are you

1: How You Keep Yourself Stuck in Drama and How to Get Out

persecuting? Are you not again persecuting yourself?

A third type of dream persecution occurs when you wake up in a dream by becoming lucid, that is, aware during the dream that you are dreaming, and change it according to your wishes without considering the interests of the other characters in the dream. To understand how this is abuse, switch roles. How do you feel when people come into your life and demand that they change to meet your expectations? While IDL has nothing against lucid dreaming, one of the reasons it teaches deep listening to dream characters is so that your lucidity can support the agenda of your life compass instead of simply colonizing your dream world with your own waking agenda.

A final way that you may be abusive in your dreams is occurs when you jump to conclusions, based on the assumption that your perspective and assessment of dream events is correct, without stopping to ask questions of other dream characters. For example, most dream monsters and villains, when questioned either during dreams or afterward, during an IDL interview, will tell you that their intent was beneficent: to wake you up to get you to pay attention to something that they consider important that you are ignoring. Because you are ignoring normal wake-up calls, the next step is to startle or scare you awake in an attempt to get you to pay attention. Instead, this strategy normally fails, because you assume you are being persecuted and respond with persecution or self-rescuing, both of which miss the message and perpetuate the Drama Triangle.

Persecution in your dreams matters because it reinforces anxiety, depression, hopelessness, and helplessness that are probably already strong elements in your life script. Dream self-persecution makes it more difficult for you to function in your daily life or to use the help of counselors, coaches, and spiritual teachers to get unstuck.

How do you know when you are in the role of Persecutor? When you yell, blame, attempt to make others feel guilty, manipulate others to get them to do what you want them to do, interrupt, name-call, gossip, drive aggressively or tell people what is real and true for them and what they should do, you are in the role of Persecutor. Stop rationalizing your actions and face that reality and what it means. The role of Persecutor is in the eye of the beholder, which generally means you need to learn to respect the opinion of those who claim to be the victim of abuse by you. Give them the benefit of the doubt. However, a more accurate and effective way of telling if you are in the role of persecutor or not is to ask, "What is the opinion of objective others who don't have a bias one way or the other?" For example, in a dispute between a parent and a child or between partners, the perspective of a counselor is often more trustworthy because it is more objective. In a dispute between nations, an international court is often more objective and trustworthy. You will learn below how IDL interviewing provides you with powerful internal sources of objectivity in the form of the perspectives of dream characters and personifications of life issues that you interview. Since Persecutors are naturally blind to their own abusiveness, if anyone tells you that you are in the role of Persecutor, ask for more information. Assume that they may be correct, even if you don't see it.

That does *not* mean is that you should therefore blame yourself or feel guilty. This is what people fear and desperately attempt to avoid, generally by changing the subject to the behavior of others, that is, by blaming others instead. But this is a false choice. Both blaming others *and* blaming yourself keep you stuck in the Drama Triangle. You persecute yourself whenever you think, "I'm stupid, ugly or a failure." "I can't do it," "They'll never like me," "It will never work," or "I'm to blame." Recognizing these cognitive distortions and learning to substitute realistic and accurate alternative thoughts is an essential life skill to protect yourself from depression and anxiety. Whenever you are critical of others or yourself, you are probably functioning in the role of Persecutor.

Tornadoes, earthquakes, floods and man-eating tigers are not in the role of Persecutors. That involves motives we project onto them that they do not have. Similarly, very young children are not persecutors because they are enmeshed in their sensory and emotional environments prior to an awareness of the Drama Triangle.

While there are circumstances where consequences can be delivered without being in the role of Persecutor, assume you are not smart enough to know the difference and that no one else is, either. Assume that those who say that some action you find abusive is not persecution are probably indulging in some form of self-justification. A good example is self-criticism. While you may be willing to acknowledge that this is a form of persecution, you justify it because you think you *deserve* it. Isn't this a rationalization and an excuse? Is it persecution or not? Isn't it self-persecution, whether you think you deserve it or not? Just because you are stuck in the role of persecutor, this does not mean you are justified in persecuting yourself for it! Blaming yourself only perpetuates your suffering and keeps you stuck in the Drama Triangle. It is much more effective to ask yourself some questions in a level-headed sort of way:

"When do I play the role of Persecutor?"

"When I find myself persecuting others, what do I do?"

"When I find myself persecuting myself, what do I do?"

"How is that working for me?"

"If I have a job or role that "forces" me into the role of Persecutor, how long am I willing to accept that excuse for staying stuck in the Drama Triangle?"

"Do I want to stop enough to give up my excuses and change my behavior?"

If you want to stop, you can.

You need objectivity to wake you up out of persecution because you don't realize that's what you're doing. As you read on, you will find powerful ways that IDL can help you get and use the objectivity you need to recognize and stop falling into the Persecutor role of the Drama Triangle.

The Role of Victim

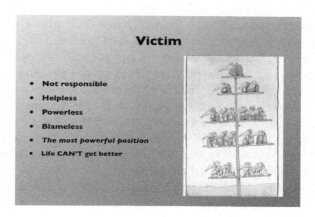

We all get victimized by disease, accidents, aging and each other. Shit happens. However, being victimized is different from being in the role of Victim. Victims are helpless, hopeless and powerless. Therefore, they are blameless and not responsible. Victims say, "It's all those bad Persecutors that have to be dealt with before I can ever be happy." These Persecutors are not limited to other people. They may be debts, an illness or disability, a messy desk, a run-down house, a bad neighborhood, a corrupt government or an unhealthy environment. Because there will always be circumstances to be seen as Persecutors, life *can't* get better. Even in good times, we know that it is just a matter of time before we as Victims are abused again.

Ironically, the role of Victim is the most powerful position in the Drama Triangle. This is because Victims are blameless and so cannot change or be expected to change. In divorces, it's generally the other person's fault that the marriage didn't work out. If you get fired, it's because your boss is unfair. If you don't get the job you want, it's because the system is rigged. Prisons are full of people who are convinced they are Victims, quite apart from whether they were victimized or not. As we shall see, some people spend their entire lives imagining they are Victims of their actions in past lives, meaning they persecute themselves for everything. It is their "karma." At the other extreme, Israel, Zionism, and Judaism all generally use chronic Victim status for self protection by professing perpetual victimization and therefore non-responsibility for whatever actions they are therefore compelled to take to defend themselves. The result is resentment, because no one likes being seen as helpless, hopeless, and powerless, followed by self-rescuing, followed by the generation of more Persecutors.

Victims are chronically, perpetually depressed. Because most people are stuck in the Drama Triangle, most people are depressed, living lives of what Thoreau called "quiet desperation." If you put on a happy face and have a lot of energy and still feel powerless and out of control, trapped on the squirrel-wheel of life, then you're depressed and stuck in the Drama Triangle. That's the existential position most people find themselves in most of the time.

In the domain of interpersonal relations and your cultural-social reality, you are in the Victim role of the Drama Triangle when you perceive yourself, fairly or unfairly persecuted by people, events, governments, genes, demons, or deities. In the domain of cognition, you put yourself in the Victim role of the Drama Triangle when you take self-abuse. This means listening to and accepting self-critical thoughts, scare yourself, or attempt to punish yourself. In the domain of dreams, you put yourself in the Victim role when you allow yourself to be persecuted by your own self-created delusions. All three of these domains are interdependent; if you work to get out of one and ignore the other two you will be much less successful. You need to learn to interrupt patterns of victimization in all three domains. However, the good news is working on getting out of one will make it easier for you to get out of the other two.

To get out of the Victim role, you have to decide that just because you get victimized, you aren't going to play the role of Victim. You have to face the fact that you are addicted to the Drama Triangle and are stuck in the role of Victim and continuously search for self-rescuing or rescuing by others, vacations, an increase in income or retreat into cyber-fantasy. You need to recognize that you can have no deep inner peace of mind or lasting happiness in the role of the Victim. Playing the Victim not only does not help, it only makes victimization worse. You also have to decide that victimization does not give you the right to play the role of the Persecutor. Beyond that, you need to understand that attempting to escape hopelessness and helplessness by jumping into self-righteous anger only keeps you trapped in the Drama Triangle.

When do you play the role of Victim? How is that working for you? When you find yourself victimizing yourself, what do you do? When you find yourself seeing others as Victims, what do you do? Are you ready to give up your excuses for staying stuck in the role of the Victim?

The Role of Rescuer

1: How You Keep Yourself Stuck in Drama and How to Get Out

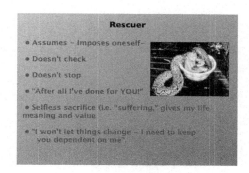

Victims need Rescuers; they are perpetually looking for them and, if they can't find them, they'll manufacture them, creating gurus, messiahs, saviors, life-saving technologies like bioresonance and Oberon, and soul-mates. Victims attempt to escape their hopelessness and helplessness by rescuing themselves by escaping into mindless and addictive avoidance strategies like smoking, drinking, eating junk food, gambling, watching TV, working to avoid family and personal conflict, reading escapist novels or taking vacations to "get away from it all." It's easy to feel you need to be rescued from your fears, your depression, your lack of control, your insecurity or the boring monotony of your stressful day-to-day life. Another strategy for self-rescue is to find meaning in your life by rescuing others by becoming either a professional or an *ad hoc* rescuer. Who is to say that self-rescuing, rescuing others or being rescued by others is not better than staying stuck? Of course it is! That is not the issue, however. The question is, do you have any viable, better alternatives to Rescuing within the Drama Triangle?

Rescuers are not selfless at all; instead, they are selfish because they are attempting to help themselves but are being dishonest about it by making the rescue effort seem like it is all about self-sacrifice to benefit the other person. If the person they are "helping" asks them to stop or complains that they aren't being helped or listened to, the rescuer is likely to think, if not actually say, "After *all* I've done for you! *This* is the thanks I get!" Rescuers end up feeling over-worked and under-appreciated, on the road to burn-out. Secretly, they don't want to stop rescuing. It allows them to feel secure and adequate by keeping others dependent on them. Moms that build their lives around their children are classic examples of rescuers. If the child favors the father or doesn't make the life decisions that the mother wants, she feels betrayed. When the child leaves home, her life is empty, because she has no life of her own; she has been living vicariously through her child.

1: How You Keep Yourself Stuck in Drama and How to Get Out

Persecutors typically think they are Helpers. They masquerade their cruelty by thinking, "I'm only doing this for your own good." "I am killing these people to keep my country safe." Victims often rescue themselves through avoidance, "tuning out," and anesthetizing themselves with food, TV, the internet, shopping, drugs, sex and endless drama—anything that changes the subject away from their inner emptiness and fear of failure. You get to choose most of what you do, think or feel during any twenty-four-hour period. Even when you are at work, you get to choose how you think and feel about your work. If you look at your life in this way, you will see that almost everything you do is a self-rescuing behavior. You are either rescuing yourself from boredom, work and responsibilities you don't want to do, the presence of interfering family members or co-workers, or your own internal self-critical, persecuting voices. Perhaps you are rescuing yourself from your fear that you are a failure or that life is meaningless. You may work to rescue yourself from fear of poverty, of failing, or to avoid some terrible home situation. You are afraid to stop, because you don't know where or how to find meaning in your life outside the Drama Triangle. Minding your parents was supposed to rescue you from their punishment; school was supposed to rescue you from failure and ridicule; work was supposed to rescue you from poverty; relationships were supposed to rescue you from loneliness. How has that worked out for you? If rescue and self- rescue is the reality you've lived with all your life you may not be able to imagine anything else. You may well be suspicious of those who claim that there might really be an alternative.

IDL encourages your suspicions. However, it also encourages you to temporarily suspend your disbelief for your own self-interest. Why? Because if you do not, you will continue to do what you have always done and get the same results you have always gotten. You will stay stuck. If you play the Rescuer, will you not inevitably be viewed as a Persecutor by others, because you aren't listening to them, instead imposing your idea of what they need? Consequently, will you not eventually end up feeling like an unappreciated Victim yourself.

1: How You Keep Yourself Stuck in Drama and How to Get Out

The role of Rescuer in relationships should be pretty clear by now. Do you also see how most of the behaviors you do are largely attempts to rescue yourself from something, like your to-do list, or from some unpleasant feeling or responsibility? Regarding your night time dreams, don't you rescue yourself when you don't remember them so you don't have to look at the internal reality you have created for yourself? Do you also rescue yourself in your dreams when you make them mean what you want them to mean instead of listening to what the characters may have to tell you? You can also stay stuck in the role of Rescuer while you are dreaming by changing the dream to avoid some threat, dreaming a different one, which is like changing the channel on your TV, or waking up in order to avoid some dream event.

When do you play the role of Rescuer? How is that working for you? When you find yourself rescuing yourself, what do you do? When you find yourself rescuing others, what do you do? Are you ready to identify your self-rescuing thoughts, feelings and behaviors, so you can get on the road to happiness and inner peace that you deserve?

What Makes the Drama Triangle a Game?

There are at least two factors that make the Drama Triangle a game. First and foremost, it's dishonest. Games have ulterior motives. Whatever role you play, you are being inauthentic unless you are consciously choosing to play that role, and healthy people do not consciously choose to be an Persecutor, Rescuer, or Victim. If you are consciously choosing to play one of these roles, you are being manipulative, which is also dishonest, unless the other players have agreed to assume such roles as well, as occurs in theatre, board games, and athletics.

There is a second, tricky distinction, and that is when Helpers take on roles to be of service. You may well be perceived in the Drama Triangle, when you are not;

the challenge is to not justify whatever you do in terms of some higher purpose: persecution in the name of God as a "Just War:" rescuing and persecuting in the name of love, Christ and God as colonizing Christianity has done; or playing the victim/martyr as soldiers and sacrificing parents may do.

Secondly, in both games and the Drama Triangle you inevitably switch roles. If you play one role, you will eventually play them all. If you play the Rescuer you will inevitably be seen as a Persecutor and eventually feel Victimized. For example, parents routinely try to help their children with homework or being on time and are met with snarls, because they are perceived as Persecutors. Have they gotten permission or understanding from their children that their function is a helpful one? If they have not, parents are likely to feel themselves Victims of persecuting children. The moral of the story is: play any of these three roles and you'll eventually play all three. While everyone seems to think that they have figured out how to defy this universal psychological law, it is an easy principle to test. When you find yourself feeling victimized by your spouse, children, employer, friends, co-workers, government or biology, ask yourself, "Would this "Persecutor" do the same if I wasn't here and someone else was doing the same thing in relation to them?" If the answer is "yes," then the "persecution" is not about you. Therefore, it is a misperception to take it personally and feel victimized.

While a businessman may think, "I'll rip off my customers, offshore jobs, and exploit the environment and get away with it," they themselves are generally blind to the fact that they are in the role of the Persecutor. They generally see themselves as offering valuable services or even doing "God's work," like President George Bush or Lloyd Blankfein of Goldman Sachs. They see others as unappreciative of their "sacrifice," and themselves as victims of the selfishness of others. To the extent that we choose to live our lives within the Drama Triangle we block our personal development through our personalization and taking too much or too little responsibility.

2: *Freeing Yourself from the Drama Triangle*

Psychological drama is emotional and personal investment in a role. When you are in one of your customary life roles, such as parent, spouse, boss, employee, or friend, if something happens in your role that you do not like, you are likely to think it is happening to *you*. This is a profound, fundamental, and pervasive misperception that creates untold misery not only in your waking life but in your dreams as well. It is a fundamental emotional cognitive distortion, called *personalization* that is based on the perceptual cognitive distortion called "psychological geocentrism," which assumes that you are the center of reality, in that whatever happens is about *you*. Such a delusion automatically puts you in the role of Victim in the Drama Triangle. When bad things happen, they are due to someone or something else. Victims refuse to accept responsibility, thinking, "Why does this always happen to ME?" Victims feel helpless, powerless, and out of control.

Alternately, Victims love to wallow in their own incompetence, wailing, "It's all MY fault!" "I'm no good!" "I'll never amount to anything!" Rescuers think they are putting the needs of others before their own. They think are just helping others out of the kindness of their heart, but they are not. A Persecutor is an abuser. Abusers treat others in ways that they would not want to be treated. They say, "You need to be punished and I'm going to punish you!" "I'll do so by blaming, scapegoating, attacking, or ignoring you." You are in the role of Persecutor when you put your needs before the needs of others and do not take

2: Freeing Yourself from the Drama Triangle

their needs into consideration.

What are the Differences Between a Rescuer and a Helper?

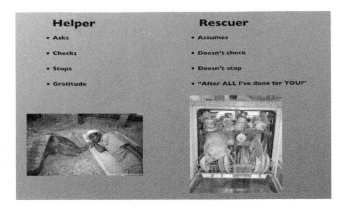

To get out of the Drama Triangle you need to understand the differences between a Rescuer and a Helper. A Rescuer assumes that their help is needed and jumps in without asking for permission while a Helper waits for a request. For example, one woman called the fire department to rescue a cat that was meowing in a tree. The fireman on the other end of the line said, "Lady, have you ever seen a cat skeleton in a tree?" The cat didn't need rescuing; that was a projection by the concerned lady. People who finish your sentences for you or interrupt think they are Helpers when they are rescuing themselves. Rescuers "keep on keeping on" without checking to see if their help is appropriate or actually making things better. When I was a boy my mother would ask me at the dinner table if I would like some more and then pile more on my plate regardless of what I answered. Rescuers just assume that what they are giving is what is needed or desired. Rescuers also don't stop when the job is done. They assume that they have permission to assist in other ways when they don't. For example, if you ask your mother for a new bedspread she may furnish your entire apartment for you, to her taste and then be shocked if you aren't appreciative. The refrain of Rescuers is, "I work so hard and nobody ever appreciates me!" "After ALL I've done for YOU!!!" If you have ever felt this way, it's a sure tip-off that you were playing the role of Rescuer. You're on the road to burn-out.

The reward rescuers get for being so caring, committed, and self-sacrificing is they burn out. They give until they have nothing else to give and then collapse emotionally, mentally, physically, or all three. When they burn out they switch

2: Freeing Yourself from the Drama Triangle

from Rescuer to Victim, persecuted by all those who have not rewarded them for their altruism and self-sacrifice.

Rescuers burn out because they give more than they get. This is because they are not honest about what they need. Their premise is, "If I give and give, everybody will love me, appreciate me, treat me nice, and love and care for me." When people do not read this unspoken script and instead take what is freely given without any request for reciprocity, they are shocked and often feel manipulated when they find that all this giving wasn't so altruistic after all, that all the time there were unspoken expectations, and that now they are being blamed for the health crisis of the poor, overworked, under-appreciated Rescuer. I must admit my first training-wheel marriage was like that. Lacking self-confidence, I married a young lady with a number of fears. I could validate my own self-worth by helping her get rid of them. When I did she was supposed to be grateful and express her appreciation by caring for my needs. When I started asking to have my needs met she was not responsive. Why should she be? That wasn't the contract! I was supposed to give and she was supposed to get! My rescuing landed me first in the role of Persecutor and then, naturally, eventually in the role of Victim.

If Rescuers sound dishonest to you, that's because they are. They give to others in order to validate their own life script, which is something like, "If I am loving, generous, and caring, other people will be loving, generous, and caring to me." Parents and society have a strong vested interest in teaching children this script because they grow up to be obedient, compliant, respectful grunts. They cause no problems, and if there are problems, if you blame them they will take responsibility and jump in and try to fix them, even if you caused the problem in the first place. If this description fits you and makes you angry, that means you are on the road to recovery. A little focused, directed anger can be a healthy thing when it is channeled in constructive rather than abusive ways. You're waking up!

We have to learn how to distinguish the imposition of structures we don't like but need from Persecutors, Helpers from Rescuers and victimization, as in car crashes and disease, from the role of Victim. These are lessons that each of us has to learn for ourselves. It is not easy, because human nature seeks rescuing in countless ways: comfort food, avoidance of responsibility, messiahs, soul mates, altered states of consciousness, vacations, the internet, an imagined future, sleep, hobbies, sex, status, wealth, validating groups, belief systems, dreams, mystical experiences, meditation, love, and meaningful relationships. None of these things are in themselves Rescuers, and all of them are often used to rescue ourselves. Consequently, it is wisdom to get into the habit of asking, "If I were using what I am doing/thinking/feeling right now to rescue me from something, what would it be?" The answer to that question is generally both revealing and important.

Why do we chronically seek rescuing? Why do we continuously seek to rescue ourselves? We do so to the extent that we experience ourselves in the role of Victim: hopeless, helpless, powerless, incapable, defenseless, vulnerable, and out of control. And so we compensate for that fear of inadequacy by throwing ourselves into relationships, activities, thoughts, and feelings that reassure us that we really are "OK." But because these activities are avoidance strategies, we are merely fueling the problem of escape from real or imagined Persecutors.

What is the solution? Part of it is to learn to deeply listen to ourselves in an integral sort of way. We need to ask, "Am I really being persecuted, or is it a delusion, like the monsters and threats I create in my nightmares?" "Am I really a Victim, or is this just a habitual belief I use to protect me from the fear of failure

2: Freeing Yourself from the Drama Triangle

if I stand up and shout out to the world who I am?" "Do I really need rescuing, or is that just my addiction to escapism and avoidance talking?" "If I choose not to listen to it, what will happen?"

Integral Deep Listening proposes that you perform experiments that will free you from the chronic, self-generated misery and suffering of the Drama Triangle. The easiest and best way to do this is to find and become authentic perspectives or points of view that aren't stuck in the Drama Triangle like you are. The more you become such perspectives the more unstuck you become. This is a major reason why IDL recommends you interview and become the characters in your dreams and the personifications of your life issues. This causes you to access perspectives that include, yet transcend, your own, and which are typically less enmeshed in the Drama Triangle than you are.

The more you do so, the more you wake up. The more you move out of misery and suffering and into freedom from the real tyrants of the world: your own self-created delusions. As a result you become more clear and free to offer your many talents to the world. Both humanity and life itself need you to free yourself. Now, more than ever, the world needs your unique gifts.

How Separation of Roles Keeps You Stuck in the Drama Triangle

In your waking life, you switch roles, for instance from sleeper to dresser to commuter to worker to cook to relaxer over time. This keeps you from experiencing the inconsistencies and conflicts among roles since they are separated by time and function. You could go to work at the National Security Agency spying on people and come home and be a dedicated partner and parent without any apparent cognitive dissonance because of this separation of your life roles by time and function. This separation of roles can even keep you from realizing that you are playing one or another of the roles of the Drama Triangle.

Dreams intensify the Drama Triangle by collapsing the three roles of Rescuer, Victim, and Persecutor into one time with multiple personifications. You experience yourself in all three roles but with this critical difference: you experience yourself in all three roles *at the same time* in the context of other parts of yourself. If you dream of a roaring fire about to consume you, you are the Victim of yourself as the fire, which is your role as Persecutor. You take the role of your Rescuer when you escape or put out the fire, change to another dream or wake up. Therefore, when you play one role, you play them all; when you experience another dream character as playing the role of persecuting monster, you are merely scaring and persecuting yourself.

IDL speeds up the process of stopping the Drama Triangle by depicting where you are stuck in Drama Triangles in your life. As we will see below in Margo's dream of cancer, if you are playing the Rescuer, Victim, or Persecutor in your life you will have dream characters giving voice to these roles in your dreams. As you listen to them and neutralize these internal conflicts with wisdom, empathy, and inner peace, you will stop externalizing your internal dramas as waking life dramas.

3: The Drama Triangle in the Three Realms:
An Integral Retelling of Dukkha

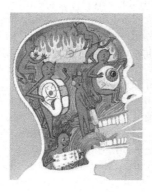

We all grew up on cartoons that portrayed one example of the Drama Triangle after another. Some villain is persecuting someone or some group of people and a hero appears, who after many trials, failures and mistakes rescues the Victim and defeats the Persecutor. If we were readers, we may have encountered the Harry Potter series in which Drama Triangles play out within Drama Triangles. Later, we may have explored the Drama Triangle further with Tolkein's *Lord of the Rings* or *Pride and Prejudice*. Greek mythology, in fact all mythologies, are retellings of the Drama Triangle in endless variations. Growing up, we were encountering the Drama Triangle in the world of our imagination when we were not confronting it in our relationships with our parents, siblings, peers and teachers. As adults we are enmeshed in the Drama Triangle with our families, at work, in government and in geopolitics, whether or not we are aware that this is the case.

What makes something as predictable as the Drama Triangle so captivating? Don't we know that in these stories that in all probability good will conquer evil, love will overcome hate and selfishness, and justice will win out over injustice? When it does not, as in *Oedipus Rex* or *Othello*, we revel in the horror of noble people coming undone, generally by their own naivete, ignorance or stupidity. We know that could be our fate, and we fear it yet are drawn to it, like a moth to a flame.

Any life issue you have may work its way out in drama in all three of the realms of your everyday reality, your relationships, thinking and night-time dreams. Imagine you are late for an appointment. You show up and your partner or friend says, "You're an hour late! You didn't even call! Can't you ever be on time?" You feel like a Victim because you hear her persecuting you. You look for some way to rescue yourself and perhaps the night out. You have multiple options. You could counter-attack, saying something clever like, "At least I dress nicely instead of showing up looking like Dobby the House Elf." You could change the subject: "We need to hurry or we'll miss the show!" You could apologize and grovel appropriately: "I'm so sorry, darling. I know I'm late again." You could come up with a clever excuse: "Someone got hit by a car and I had to administer CPR for an hour!" You could outright lie and make it the other person's fault at the same time: "You said we were to meet at 7:30, not 7:00!" You could play psychologist: "You sound really angry. If I were you I would be really angry too." You could play indignant child: "Well! If that's the way you're going to be you can just go by yourself!"

The important thing is to realize that almost anything and everything you do in such a situation is probably going to be some attempt at rescuing yourself, the other person, the situation or all of the above. The problem with rescuing within the Drama Triangle is that it often works. Things get better. You succeed in successfully changing the subject from you behavior to theirs or to some other subject; you succeed in getting them to accept your apology or excuse.

At the same time the Drama Triangle is being strengthened in your relationship it is going on in your head. You are worried about getting criticized for being late (Persecutor and Victim roles, depending on which player you are) and thinking up something to say to rescue yourself or the situation. Your thoughts are reinforcing the Drama Triangle unless you are aware of it and take steps to counteract it.

You go home and go to sleep, just wanting to forget all about it. Guess what you dream about? Most dreams deal, at least in part, with problem solving around those issues that were conflictual during your day, with those that generated the most intense emotionality most likely to work their way into your dream content. What sorts of waking issues are most likely to generate the most emotional ambivalence? Are they not those issues that most intensively act out the Drama Triangle? Are they not those that most intensively act it out in both relationships and in your thinking?

Consequently, you are very likely to spend your time dreaming metaphorical presentations of analogous persecutions, victimizations and self-rescuings in an attempt to resolve or neutralize those issues. So, for instance, those with PTSD replay as nightmares the nightmare scenarios of their waking fears. However, your dreams essentially reinforce drama rather than resolve it because they are framed within the Drama Triangle within your dream, as they are in your waking life and in your thinking,. The solutions that are provided within your dreams are very likely to occur within the context of drama, merely reinforcing your victimization within the Drama Triangle.

Based on years of observing the transformations of dream content of those who have worked with IDL, recognizing and neutralizing the Drama Triangle in your relationships and thinking will definitely reduce its prominence in your dreams. However, this process will be both reinforced and speeded up if you also take steps to more directly reduce the Drama Triangle in your dreams themselves. This is a form of lucid dreaming that is different from realizing while you are dreaming that you are asleep and dreaming; it is a lucidity that involves recognizing invitations into the Drama Triangle and saying "no thanks." This becomes more likely when pre-sleep suggestion is used, but more importantly, when IDL is used to interview dream Persecutors, Rescuers and Victims the result is an objectification of the Drama Triangle in a way that not only reduces its frequency and intensity while dreaming, but in the other two realms of relationships and thinking.

Integral Deep Listening (IDL) understands the Drama Triangle, consisting of the three interdependent and co-arising roles of Persecutor, Victim and Rescuer, as a modern and psychological reframing of the ancient and classical sources of human misery: *avidya,* or ignorance, *maya,* or illusion, *karma,* or self-generated captivity or suffering, and *sin,* or separation from God, the common explanation for human misery in the three Western monotheisms. The Drama Triangle can also be understood as a contemporary reconceptualization of the Hindu and Buddhist concept of *dukkha,* o r suffering, anxiety, frustration or distress. According to these traditions, suffering is inherent to the human condition. Gotama said, "...it is only suffering that I describe, and the cessation of suffering. " I n Hinduism the solution is *moksha,* freedom, from *samsara* or illusion, reincarnation and rebirth. In Buddhism, *dukkha* arises from birth, aging, illness and dying and from having that which is not desirable. Buddha said, "Long is the night for the sleepless. Long is the road for the weary. Long is samsara (the cycle of continued rebirth) for the foolish, who have not recognized the true teaching." In the *Padmasambhava* it is written, "All beings have lived and died and been reborn countless times. Over and over again they have experienced the indescribable Clear Light. But because they are obscured by the darkness of ignorance, they wander endlessly in a limitless samsara." Suffering also arises from not getting what you want and from the changing nature of all things as well as when life does not measure up to our expectations or standards.

For the *Advaita Vedanta* Hinduism of Shankara, the solution to *dukkha* is recognition of one's true identity, *Atman,* or Self, as one with divinity, or *Brahman.* Shankara: "To be free from bondage the wise person must practice discrimination between One-Self and the ego-self. By that alone you will become full of joy, recognizing Self as Pure Being, Consciousness and Bliss." Buddhism emphasizes the recognition of *annata,* or "no self," meaning the non-existence of any permanent self or state whatsoever. "Body is not self, feelings are not self, perception is not self, mental constructs are not self and consciousness is not self...When one sees this one becomes detached from these things, being detached the passions fade, when the passions have faded one is free, and being free one knows one is free."[1] In both cases, wisdom replaces chronic ignorance and leads to freedom from attachments that generate karma and reincarnation.

We can see from the above that for Hinduism and Buddhism suffering is a metaphysical and religious problem that therefore requires metaphysical and religious solutions. *Atman, Brahman, dharma, maya, karma* and reincarnation are all faith and experiential-based beliefs that do not require reason but do require the embracing of a particular and non-secular world view. The soul, spirituality and God, concepts recognized by both Indian and Western religious traditions, are also metaphysical concepts, largely non-falsifiable. Consequently they are faith-based and prepersonal, as are religious beliefs and mythologies.

The question becomes, "Are prepersonal faith-based framings still adequate today?" The answer is, "Yes, for some, but not so much for others." This is because such concepts tend to create a chasm between believers and non-believers, the sacred and the secular, the holy and the profane, the pure and the contaminated, the non-discriminatory and the rednecks, splitting the world into a dualism of the sanctified and the "deplorables." The world has witnessed how such distinctions inevitably bring not only personal development but societal consensus to a screeching halt.

The reason has to do with the rise of modernism and reason, standards of validity based on consensus and repeatability, and increasing skepticism since the 1700's. Increasingly, belief is not enough; people who think demand that beliefs be reasonable, that is, that in addition to being inspiring and useful, that they make sense. Unlike St. Augustine, contemporary man is less likely to think that "Understanding is the reward of faith. Therefore, seek not to understand that you may believe, but believe that you may understand." Unlike Tertullian, modern man largely will not say, "I believe because it is absurd." Instead, he asks, "Why should I believe?" "Is there a reliable foundation on which to ground my belief and if so, what is it?" "How do you know what you claim you know?" "Yes, what you say is fascinating and I can see it helps you and a lot of other people. And does it make sense?"

Many factors have driven modern man to these questions and it looks like they

---

1 (Samyutta Nikaya 3. 66)

are not going to go away. Therefore, bridges need to be built between traditional and belief/experience-based concepts like *dukkha* and the contemporary world of secular rationality. IDL uses the Drama Triangle as such a bridge, attempting to honor the contributions of both belief and reason, sacred and secular domains to create a broader foundation for how and why there is suffering and what we can do to extract ourselves from it.

The concept of the Drama Triangle, as originally formulated and normally understood, is not a good reconceptualization of *dukkha*, primarily because it addresses only relationships, one of four equally important aspects of the human condition. In the holonic model of Integral AQAL, created by Ken Wilber, relationship co-creates reality with behavior, value or culture, and interior consciousness, including our thoughts and feelings. It does so in different stages of development as well as in different states, chief among them being waking, dreaming, deep sleep and altered states of consciousness, as notably represented by mystical and near death experiences. An integral retelling of *dukkha* will therefore not only be post-metaphysical and falsifiable, but will be mindful of how drama is reframed developmentally as we grow. It will also consider how the Drama Triangle shows up in our interior world in various states, something its original interpersonal formulation by Transactional Analysis does not emphasize.

There indeed exist interpersonal aspects of the Drama Triangle in our thoughts and dreams, since thoughts and feelings that get us in and out of drama interact both in our thinking and dreaming, it can equally be said that behavior, value and interior consciousness pervade the interpersonal realm. Which is most important? Integral approaches such as IDL respond that the one we are forgetting, or the one which is least integrated in a particular moment of drama, is the most important. Therefore, for IDL, the Drama Triangle takes into account not only drama in thinking, interpersonal relationships and dreaming, but also its relationship to the dimensions of personal behavior and values. We address the relationship between the Drama Triangle and values in our chapter on *The Drama Triangle as a Perceptual Cognitive Distortion* as well as in its relationship to one antidote, the Socratic Triune.

The Drama Triangle is not native to Integral or AQAL, just as it is not part of man's religious-spiritual heritage. It is a secular-humanist concept most closely associated with choice-based approaches to humanistic psychology and has remained closely associated with Transactional Analysis, from which it sprang. While it has been adapted to various interpersonal applications in human relations and business,[2] it has remained closely associated with both

---

2   Counseling applications: social welfare, health care, pastoral work, prevention, mediation, process facilitation, multicultural work, and humanitarian activities;

Transactional Analysis and interpersonal relationships.[3] However, it has much broader applications, and one of the purposes of this book is to call some of them to the attention of the reader.

The Drama Triangle in an Integral Context

We have already noted that the Drama Triangle can be observed in any and all states of consciousness, but chiefly in waking, thinking and dreaming. Because thinking is a process that occurs in all states and therefore is not itself a state, IDL uses the term "realms" instead of states. Another purpose of this usage is to not imply that there are only three states that the Drama Triangle can be associated with. For instance, if you read descriptions of near death experiences you will often find rescuing figures and experiences; people can come away from near death experiences perceiving life as a Persecutor in a way that they never had before. They may experience themselves as a victim of incarnation in their physical body, an awareness that moves them into a state of existential depression in which they go sour on a life that now seems to have little or no meaning when compared with the indescribable magnificence of their near death

---

Educational transactional analysis applications include working in training centers, preschools, elementary and high schools, universities, and institutions that prepare teachers and trainers as well as in support of learners of all ages to thrive within their families, organizations, and communities; Organizational transactional analysis applications include using its concepts and techniques to evaluate an organization's developmental processes and challenges as well as its dysfunctional behaviors.

3 For example, Berne, E., *Games People Play;* Harris, T.A., *I'm OK, You're OK,* Steiner, C., *Scripts People Live,* James, M. & Jongeward, D.,*Born to Win.*

2: Freeing Yourself from the Drama Triangle

or mystical experience.

IDL also differentiates "thinking" as a separate "realm" because it represents the internal individual quadrant of consciousness of the human holon.[4] What we think about our experience and what we actually experience, whether in waking life or a dream, is not only often different, but the realm of thought can be abstracted from both to much benefit, as is done with the investigation and elimination of cognitive distortions, following Beck and Burns. How we think about our dreams both when we are dreaming and afterward, when we are awake, is clearly at least as important as dreaming itself. How we structure our thoughts about our relationships is at least as important as our relationships themselves, because those thoughts largely determine the course of those relationships.

It is clear that dreams spring up independent of out thoughts or we would know what they mean and why we have them. At best we make calculated guesses about the meaning of our dreams that feel like they could be true, but how do we know? Because the inherent nature of visual metaphor is ambiguity of meaning, our meanings or interpretations remain partial at best and often well wide of the mark, as we can easily determine with IDL interviewing.

It is also clear that our dreams contain significant amounts of drama; one could contend that dreaming is *mostly* drama. Therefore, we find endless retelling of the Drama Triangle in dream reality. We will also
see that dreaming is hardly a distinct and separate realm; the depth of our enmeshment in drama in our dreams has pervasive and long-term consequences for our physical and mental health as well as for our relationships.

The Drama Triangle evolves as we do. When we are children reality is external and concrete; the Drama Triangle appears primarily in our external relationships with others. However, for those who look at the dreams of children, it is obvious that their dreams are filled with the Drama Triangle. Most children can easily be taught to see the three roles in their dreams, and this is itself a powerful tool for developing objectivity regarding introspection from an early age.

As we get older, the Drama Triangle takes on hues, colorations, and depth that was missed when we were younger. Persecutors are no longer just bad, selfish or

---

[4]
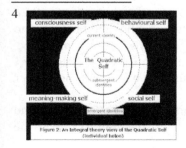

Figure 2: An Integral theory view of the Quadratic Self (individual holon)

cruel, they are unjust, self-righteous and non-empathetic. Rescuers are no longer just saviors; they impose their will in irritating ways while professing the best of intentions. This is your typical adolescent's description of their parent, at least in the contemporary West. Victims are no longer just rejected failures but hopeless and helpless.

At later stages of development Persecutors may be seen as projecting their own self-hatred and unresolved internal conflicts onto others. Rescuers may be viewed as self-centered needy manipulators headed for burn-out. Victims may be understood to be quite powerful in their disowning of any responsibility for their suffering.

An integral retelling of the Drama Triangle will also take into account the various developmental lines or aptitudes, the chief of which are our sense of self, cognition, morality, and empathy. However, there are over twenty such lines, including proprioceptive development and physical dexterity, musicality, mathematical and communicative abilities. An integral approach to the Drama Triangle will also take into account the style or approach to development of an individual. Does he or she emphasize goals and individual achievement or community and cooperation?

By approaching the Drama Triangle as a definition of delusion in any and all states IDL can use exiting the Drama Triangle as a metaphor for the traditional religious, spiritual and metaphysical goals of enlightenment, freedom, salvation and oneness. By doing so it can take etherial and sacred concepts like the holy, spirituality, sacred, nirvana, samadhi and moksha and anchor them firmly to the rough and uneven terrain of our everyday lives, where we discover if universal love really can be translated not only into love of where we are and who we are with at this moment, but into love and tolerance of ourselves.

Escaping the Drama of State Experiences

There are plenty of ways to wake up and experience states of greater wakefulness, but most are either not sustainable or are outright toxic. These include drugs, caffein, nicotine, conversion experiences, altar calls, romance, winning the lottery, exercise, movies, good books, demonic foods (like chocolate!), traveling, surfing, and various yogas (like kundalini and tantric). The question becomes, "How do I become lucid here and now, in my mundane, secular, ho-hum reality in a developmentally solid, authentic way?" "How do I sanctify the secular?" This is the core of enlightenment, happiness, and inner peace.

This central issue tends to be overlooked or minimized by both religion and spiritual paths, East and West, because it's a hard sell. It tends to reflect the

2: Freeing Yourself from the Drama Triangle

feminine path, which is gradual, gestative, and developmental, when compared to the more intense, intentional and state-focused nature of the masculine path. The goal is androgyny – the integration of the two. Just as there is nothing sexy about androgyny for those who are gender-obsessed, here's nothing really sexy about sanctifying the secular. It's more exciting to just go straight for the Holy by inducing a mystical experience of some sort, not only by finding *sat, cit,* and *ananda* (being, consciousness, bliss) ourselves, but by groking it vicariously by learning about other people's near death experiences and mystical experiences. In contrast, watching the grass of normal development grow is never going to become a major spectator sport. Kids don't get off on watching themselves learn to walk and talk. They don't say, "Gee, today I have a little more balance than I did yesterday!" "Gee, today I learned to ask for what I want!"

Developmental growth is by nature gradual and hence not nearly as exciting as are state changes, which get much more attention than they deserve. Why? Because by nature and definition they do not last. They generate a roller coaster approach to life – highs and lows; addiction to highs, avoidance of lows. Drama. Let's have mystical experiences. Let's have sacred orgasms. Sacred orgasms are delightful! But in the context of – what? Addiction to the drama of state experiences is a sign of prepersonal through personal levels of development, the childhood, adolescence, and early adulthood of human consciousness. How you frame what you are looking for in life says more than you know about your level of development.

4: The Drama Triangle as a Perceptual Cognitive Distortion

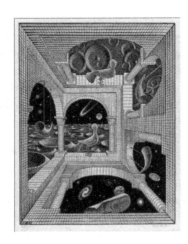

IDL recognizes three types of cognitive distortions, emotional, logical and perceptual, all of which are explained in *Waking Up*. The Drama Triangle is a perceptual cognitive distortion, that is, a world view or perceptual context that is largely invisible and that conditions what we think, feel and do, whether awake, dreaming or in some altered state of consciousness. It is invisible because we are subjectively enmeshed in it, like your lack of awareness of the space between your eyes and these words that you are now reading, or your awareness of the back of your head. Just the mention of these possibilities immediately and radically alters both your perspective and the possibilities available to you.

The nature of perceptual cognitive distortions is similar to the relationship between a two-dimensional flatworm and a three dimensional reality; a flatworm is embedded in a three-dimensional reality but it is so subjectively enmeshed in two dimensions that it can only infer the existence of something beyond. The Drama Triangle is then similar to the laws or structures that create reality for the flatworm, a perceptual cognitive distortion that allows it to function in harmony as a two-dimensional being within a multiple-dimensional reality.

As such, for IDL, and in contradiction to Buddhism, there is nothing intrinsically evil, bad or negative about suffering, *dukkha* or the Drama Triangle, just as there is nothing intrinsically destructive about the two-dimensional reality of a flatworm. Suffering and misery arise where the second and third dimensions intersect, where the world of the Drama Triangle as a perceptual cognitive distortion come into contact with a broader, more inclusive reality and generate

4: The Drama Triangle as a Perceptual Cognitive Distortion

cognitive dissonance. This is experienced as limitation and, when that limitation has consequences, it is experienced as suffering or misery.

However, misery is optional. We are not miserable when we are perfectly adapted within the Drama Triangle even though we are in a state of intrinsic delusion. We can draw an analogy to dreaming. With the exception of nightmares, we are normally not miserable while dreaming even though, when we awaken, we can say, "I was deceived! I thought I was awake and I was not! I was in a state of self-delusion!"

It is only as you wake up as a two-dimensional flat worm to a third dimension and experience different forms of disturbing incongruities between the two that you begin to recognize suffering and misery, where before an adaptive complacency reigned. This has also been called moving from unconscious incompetence to conscious incompetence – awareness that you have limitations that you were not even aware of before, like not being able to speak a foreign language or perform some new, required task at work.[5] When you are happily adapted within some manifestation of the Drama Triangle you are unconscious of your incompetence, so you feel no pain, suffering or misery. It is only as you wake up into the realization that you are incompetent and you have been unconscious of that fact, that you experience misery or *dukkha*.

The uroboros which is subjectively enmeshed, as symbolized by it eating its own tail, has now stopped, is looking around and is overwhelmed with a world of new possibilities. When you awaken to your enmeshment in drama, like the uroboros, you gain objectivity that you didn't have. You can look back and say, "Before I was comfortably asleep in a perceptual cognitive distortion. I thought I was awake and capable but now I realize that, relatively speaking, I was sleepwalking and not so capable." This throws you into a state of relative suffering as you recognize that your life is out of balance in ways that you were not even aware of before.[6]

Other important perceptual cognitive distortions include geocentrism, the assumption that the sun rises and sets around a stable, non-moving Earth, and psychological geocentrism, the assumption that your sense of self is the center of reality and that all events orbit around you. Other words for this psychological orientation are selfishness, narcissism and grandiosity, but these words tend to be morally judgmental, when psychological geocentrism is much more a statement of flat worm perception rather than a statement of lower ethical development.

---

5   Burch, N., *Four Stages for Learning Any New Skill,* Gordon Training International.
6   Such repression is a primary defense against overwhelm, change, the unknown and failure. Staying asleep, dreaming and sleepwalking have powerful adaptive advantages, which is why many people, when presented with the concept of the Drama Triangle both cannot conceive and do not want to conceive, of life outside of it.

*4: The Drama Triangle as a
Perceptual Cognitive Distortion*

Another profound perceptual cognitive distortion is the myth of the self, the belief that you are real, meaning that you have some permanent reality. All four of these perceptual cognitive distortions are normal and do not necessarily create suffering; one can live a full and healthy life within these contexts as long as they do not, like our flat worm, bump up against a broader dimension that plays by different rules. When that happens, the cognitive dissonance can become unbearable and lead one on a life-long quest to transition from a flat worm into a three-dimensional being.

Like other perceptual cognitive distortions, the Drama Triangle is self-perpetuating. It validates and reinforces itself; it creates its own rationales both for its continued existence and for you to continue to live out your life within its parameters. Indeed, if you want to outgrow the Drama Triangle you will have to pay a price, just as humanity has to pay a price to orbit the Earth and live in outer space. All perceptual cognitive distortions possess both gravity and inertia, and overcoming both means that you will have to make significant expenditures of your time, energy, patience, persistence, relationships and self-definition. Therefore, in recognition that quick and intense transformations very rarely last, first prepare yourself by getting as solid a conceptual foundation as you can regarding the nature of the Drama Triangle in all three realms. Then begin to take incremental, baby steps out of drama. Emphasize day-to-day quality, not the quantity of your growth. Remember that IDL provides you with a wide range of tools to help you in this enterprise, including the ability to access emerging potentials that are relatively free of drama and which possess the objectivity that you lack regarding what next steps are most advantageous and how to address the inevitable resistances that arise as you take them.

5: How the Drama Triangle Shows Up in The Three Realms

Your relationships, thinking and night time dreams together generate your reality. Just like the three roles of the Drama Triangle, these three realms are interdependent, creating, supporting and maintaining one another. Therefore, waking up in any one of these three realms supports waking up in the other two, and a three-pronged approach that encourages wakefulness in all three not only speeds your awakening but provides powerful prevention and antidotes for invitations into the Drama Triangle.

Your Relationships

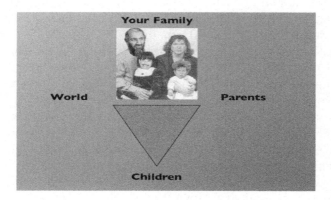

If you remember life in your childhood home, you may be able to recognize that

5: How the Drama Triangle Shows Up in The Three Realms

your parents and siblings viewed life from one or another role of the Drama Triangle most of the time. Children generally take the role of potential victims of a dangerous, impersonal, cold and persecuting world, to be protected by their rescuing parents. Parents want their children to be happy but they are afraid they won't be unless they go to school, play by the rules, learn a career and have a family.

Families that are normally in all three roles of the Drama Triangle create a toxic environment in which to raise children. The problem is not with families; the problem is that family members don't recognize when they are in the Drama Triangle and what role they are playing in it. Parents want to rescue their children from the world, because they don't have confidence that their children can learn to find and listen to their life compasses and find their own paths to fulfillment. This is understandable, because no one ever taught them the concept of life compass or how to access it, so how can parents teach it to their children? Parents don't realize that beneath all those rules for happiness that they are compelling their children to internalize lies one fundamental and toxic life skill: how to play the three roles in the Drama Triangle. All children learn how to play these three roles, and they eventually teach their children how to do so as well. Victimized by their own addiction to drama, such children grow up to exploit other families and the world itself. Parents lack the skills to get out of the Drama Triangle and stay out. Teaching them how to recognize when they are in the Drama Triangle, and how to get out and stay out are important goals of IDL.

Did you grow up in a family that was caught up in the Drama Triangle? If so, what role or roles did your mother play? When? What role or roles did your father play? When? Who generally played the persecutor in your family? Who played the rescuer? What role or roles did your siblings play? When? What role or roles did your relatives play? When? What role or role did your pets play? When? What role or roles did you play? When? Which roles do you end up playing when you are around your family? Would your other family members also see you in the same role you see yourself or in a different one?

When you talk to or visit your family members in the future, what do you need to do to keep from falling into the Drama Triangle? Remember, whether your other family members are in the Drama Triangle or not is not your problem; it is enough to recognize their plight and to avoid getting sucked into that drama yourself. If someone is covered with mud and you fight with them, you will end up covered with mud yourself. If someone is stuck in a pit and you jump in, you are stuck in the same pit with them. Your responsibility is not to get your family out of the Drama Triangle, because they may not want to change, and you don't need to put yourself in the role of rescuer. Instead, your responsibility is to ask for their help in getting out and staying out. Explain the Drama Triangle to them and invite their feedback when they think you've fallen into it. Beyond this, the

5: How the Drama Triangle Shows Up in The Three Realms

emerging potentials that you interview in IDL don't do drama. You can ask your family members to interview you as a way to help you get out of drama by getting in touch with authentic, personal antidotes to the Drama Triangle. When you ask for help from your family members, you are at the same time educating them about the Drama Triangle and introducing them to the possibility of a family culture that operates outside it. What a gift to those you love!

If you take any problem you have in your love relationships or in parenting, you can effectively look at it as an expression of your addiction to drama. For instance, your partner or kids don't listen to you. Do you feel victimized? Do you put them in the role of Persecutor? Do you want them to rescue you from this problem by growing up and learning to listen to you? Without drama, your partner or child's failure to listen will either be much less of a problem or not a problem at all. In either case, whatever is bugging you about your relationship will then be far, far easier to solve. This is the fundamental truth that gets clouded over when you start focusing on specific relationship problems, whether they involve jealousy, laziness, unfairness, infidelity, possessiveness, selfishness, stupidity, ignorance, intimidation, abuse, aggression, avoidance or some addiction. These are like limbs of a vine, like kudzu, that are smothering the tree of your love.

You can read a lot of books and spend a lot of time focusing on cutting off one or another of these limbs while ignoring the vine itself. How well is that likely to work? The trunk of the vine is your being stuck in the Drama Triangle. When you move out of the Drama Triangle, you stop fertilizing the vine that is smothering your relationship.

There are a few simple keys for doing so. Assume that whatever your partner or child says to you or about you is not about you. What they are saying or doing is stereotyped; it's stuff they learned long ago and is not about you. If you stop and think about it, wouldn't they probably say those same words to someone else if you were not in their life? This includes, yelling, name calling, interrupting, telling jokes, getting drunk, blaming, flirting, having sex with other people, buying you things—whatever. Their reality is not about you. People in drama don't love *you;* they only see the fantasized you that they have created in their own minds, based on a life of previous experiences. They have confused their delusion with you; don't compound the problem by shadow-boxing with their delusion! It may sound harsh and discounting of the genuine affection your partner has for you to say so, but you are basically a fun house mirror for your partner. They see more or less distorted aspects of themselves in you. When they talk and interact with you, they are shadowboxing with the parts of themselves that you represent. When you take what they do personally, you are making stuff that isn't about you be about you, thereby compounding the problem. Which would you prefer, dealing with their delusions or dealing with both their delusions and your delusional reactions to their delusions? Would you rather deal with one

5: How the Drama Triangle Shows Up in The Three Realms

problem or two, including a second one of your own creation?

This means you need to grow up and get over yourself. You're just not that important; you're not that special. So stop taking things personally. Start asking yourself, "Today, how personally have I taken how my partner talks and acts?"

Repeat back what your partner says. This shows that you are listening. It allows them to hear what they have said, which often leads them to clarify or correct themselves. It keeps you from reacting. It sets an example that hopefully they will emulate.

Ask questions to get more information if you are irritated or want to state your opinion. The stronger your feelings are, the more you want to state your opinion, and the more likely you are to say something that will backfire. Stall for time by asking clarifying questions. It keeps you out of drama for the moment.

Assume you are in the Drama Triangle, regardless of how sure you think otherwise. Encourage your partner to ask you, "If you were in the Drama Triangle right now, which role would you most likely be taking?" This is a sober and unpleasant question, but one you need to hear. This is not designed to leave you open to having to accept your partner's strategy of focusing on how you are playing the Persecutor/Victim/Rescuer. Your partner needs to accept their responsibility for their part in relationship drama rather than shifting the subject of the confrontation to you. Focusing on how you are in drama gives you power and control. You have power and control over the drama in your life because you created it. You get to choose how you feel. You get to be joyful if you want. You get to have peace of mind. Nobody, *nobody* is worth you giving up your peace of mind. Do you believe it?

How the Drama Triangle Destroys Personal Relationships

5: How the Drama Triangle Shows Up in The Three Realms

 The Drama Triangle is learned as part of our childhood scripting; as we watch our parents and siblings interact we learn which of the three roles to take in different circumstances. These childhood relationships form the template for who we choose as partners, how we view our partners and how we respond to their actions. The following clarifies just how powerful, pervasive and important all these relationships are.
 Tina shared the following dream: "I am a small, young lioness in a cage. There is another lion that someone threw in the cage to eat me! In fact, he starts chewing on my paw! To get him to stop I pretend I am dead and he goes off to sleep. When I think he is totally asleep I start walking around, but he wakes up! We start talking, which is really weird. The lion turns into Ralph, my husband! I tell him that whoever threw him into the cage was trying to kill me. Ralph helps me to escape from the cage, because people are trying to kill us both. He fights and conquers them. Then we evolve from lions to people. Very strange!"
 When we interviewed the cage, it told Tina that if it were in charge of her life it would give her the ability to bite her tongue when she's frustrated so she wouldn't get violent like a lion would. She would be more understanding instead of overreacting. A part of her, the other lion, is helping an evil part of her to trap and kill her. The cage advised her not to blow up whenever Ralph antagonized her because it shifted the focus from Ralph being the abuser to Tina's overreaction. It also advised her to get a job so that she would be more independent of Ralph.
 The man who put the male lion in the cage told Tina that he is a part of her that wants to keep her under its control by making her think that she can't do anything else than what she is doing. She realized that she is dependent on a critical, abusive part of herself.
 Tina said, "What I have heard myself say is that I feel like I am locked up. I feel like I have a pretty life but I can't make certain decisions and I feel trapped. Ralph feels trapped too. He was killing me; he's taken a lot out of my life. But when he realizes that he loves me, he helps both of us to escape. That may be what I really want but there are a lot of obstacles in the way of all that. I still go into rages. That takes away from anything that I do. Ralph is eating my paw. He must still be taking things away from me. He is injuring me. I want to believe that he will save me but he still hurts me.
 Tina was a very attractive nurse educator who was ten years into her second marriage and who had a fifteen-year-old daughter. She found herself in a very common predicament: financially secure with a verbally abusive and violent partner who everyone knew was having multiple affairs but that she chose to pretend weren't happening. She was miserable, but too emotionally and financially dependent to leave.
 This is a good example of the externalization of a lifelong disowned fear. In

5: How the Drama Triangle Shows Up in The Three Realms

this case, Tina was afraid of her anger hurting others. She found herself attracted to men who were strong and verbally abusive like her father was. Because she did not recognize, listen to, and evict the self-abusive part of her father that still lived rent-free inside her thoughts, this pattern was externalized in a way that could not be ignored, by embroiling her in relationships with controlling men.

Listening to her dream gave Tina an opportunity to see that she was paying all three roles of the Drama Triangle. As the man and the lion, she was abusing herself. As Ralph, she was taking turns rescuing and abusing herself. As the young lioness, Tina played the Victim. As she listened to what these parts of herself had to say, she began to understand that because she had not addressed her own internal addiction to this Drama Triangle it externalized in her relationship with her husband. However, lifelong addictions to drama are not easily overcome. This is why it is wise to interview a series of dreams and life issues over time in order to recognize when and how you function within the Drama Triangle and to reclaim as your own the power you give away to others when you imagine them in other roles in the Drama Triangle (for instance, as Persecutor or Rescuer to your Victim). From these interviews you will receive recommendations that change with your conditions and growing awareness so that you have support you need for where you are in your process of self-extraction. Work on an ongoing basis with someone who is familiar with IDL can help you choose useful recommendations from interviews, set meaningful goals, and have an accountability structure to keep you on track.

Despite her intelligence and ability to support herself, Tina dropped out of therapy and stayed with Ralph. Within two years her daughter was pregnant and the cycle started all over, passed down to yet another generation. Your addiction to both your emotional preferences and to the injunctions of your life script should never be underestimated. They will win unless you are determined, persistent and create steps to build a culture of healthy, supportive relationships that continuously offer you a realistic alternative path forward.

5: How the Drama Triangle Shows Up in The Three Realms

Your Thoughts and Feelings

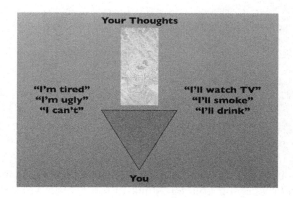

As discussed above, the Drama Triangle exists in three areas or realms of your life: your relationships, your thoughts and feelings, and in your dreams. How it shows up in your thoughts and feelings is most important, because it controls how you perceive the Drama Triangle in your outer world relationships and the inner world of your dreams. If you change how you deal with drama in your own thoughts and feelings, you will change how you deal with it in your relationships and dreams as well. Thinking within the Drama Triangle is delusional and dysfunctional. It is impossible to have peace of mind as long as you are in the Drama Triangle. It makes you sick. It causes you to feel bad. Test this statement for yourself. If you find it is true, then you are faced with a clear choice: you can either have peace of mind or you can have drama; you can't have both. All cognitive distortions occur within the Drama Triangle and cause you to live your life within it. Such cognitive distortions are a major source of depression and anxiety.

Whenever you criticize yourself, blame yourself or feel guilty, you are in the role of the Persecutor. It doesn't matter whether you think you deserve it or not; you will generally think that you do! What matters is that such thinking keeps you stuck in drama and is making you sick and crazy. Therefore, the question is not, "Do I deserve to feel bad?" but, "Is making myself feel bad keeping me stuck in the Drama Triangle or not?" When you see that such thoughts inevitably keep you stuck in a self-created delusion, dream and/or nightmare, you will start to identify your critical, blaming and guilt-producing thoughts, choose to either stop them or substitute a realistic thought, and focus on your goals rather than your weaknesses.

5: How the Drama Triangle Shows Up in The Three Realms

Whenever you use any of the various defense mechanisms you are rescuing yourself and thereby keeping yourself stuck in the Drama Triangle. For example, when you think, "One more cookie/cigarette/drink/won't hurt!" you are using a defense mechanism called "rationalization." You are rescuing yourself by creating an excuse for behavior that is a Persecutor in disguise. The result is that you keep yourself stuck in the role of Victim, feeling out of control and reacting, rather than responding to your urges, impulses, feelings and desires.

Whenever you give yourself reasons to stay stuck, you are in the role of Victim in the Drama Triangle. One of the most common ways you do this is by avoiding doing the things on your "to do" list. If you do anything on your list, you tend to do the minor and fun things and avoid the highest, most pressing priorities, because they are difficult and require more time, energy and resources. Don't you give yourself "reasons" for not doing those important things? Aren't these "reasons" merely excuses? The end result is that you feel victimized by your "to do" list! You spend your life avoiding it because you've turned it into a persecutor! Think about times when you've tackled and completed a high priority on your "to do" list. How did you feel? Didn't you feel energized? Didn't it immediately take you out of the role of the Victim?

To get out of the role of the Victim in your thoughts, observe what you are avoiding. Recognize that avoidance turns that thought, feeling or action into the Persecutor in your mind, thereby putting you in the position of Victim. Resolve to face whatever you are avoiding today and watch how you move out of the Drama Triangle.

5: How the Drama Triangle Shows Up in The Three Realms

Dreams and Nightmares

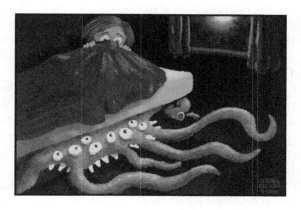

If relationships are the easiest way to spot the Drama Triangle, and thinking is the most effective way to avoid it, your night time dreams are your best guide to healing, balancing and transformation. Rightly understood, they reflect the priorities of your life compass. They provide you with the objectivity of your innate, unique center of growth that knows you better than you know yourself, better than others could possibly know you.

Most of us live within the delusion that we know who we are and what we need to do. We know we are fooling ourselves because we routinely waste precious time and money on dead-end relationships and activities like TV, games, surfing the internet, or eating junk food, that don't add to the quality of our lives in any lasting way.

Interviewing characters in your dreams and nightmares helps you to let go of your assumptions about why you had a dream and what it means and instead listen to the opinions of other authentic, innate perspectives that represent your life compass. This, in turn, helps you to let go of your assumptions about who you are and how you live your life, assumptions that are not working to bring you the growth and happiness you seek. IDL interviewing allows you to not only understand why you had a dream or a nightmare, but more importantly, you will become clearer about how and why you stay stuck and what you need to do to get unstuck. How come? IDL dream and nightmare interviews demonstrate that whether dreaming or awake, you project onto others characteristics that you yourself possess.[7] Monsters in your nightmares are recognized as your own fears. Rescuers in dreams are seen to be your own potentials. You come to understand that if you are victimized in your dreams, it is only because you are choosing to

---

7 These interviewing protocols are discussed at IntegralDeepListening.Com.

put yourself in the role of Victim; no one is doing that to you. The result is that you understand that the way you treat others is the way that you are treating those parts of yourself that they represent. You then treat others with respect, not because of social conscience, but because it shows respect for yourself. You love others not because you were taught you should be loving, but because it shows love to the part of yourself that they represent.

When you see through the drama in your dreams and nightmares, you are hearing the wake-up calls they have for you. Therefore, the self-created drama in your life tends to stop. You stop having nightmares. You stop having repetitive dreams, because you are practicing deep listening. When the Drama Triangle no longer shows up in your dreams, you have confirmation that you are no longer planting the seeds of dysfunction in your consciousness, incubating them in the soil of your inner mind while you sleep. Without seeing through the drama in your dreams, you are always vulnerable to those seeds sprouting, no matter how hard you work at eliminating the Drama Triangle from your relationships and your thoughts. Your dreams and nightmares are a continuous, enormous asset for escaping the Drama Triangle and transforming your life; are you using them?

Lucidity, Luminosity and Exiting the Drama Triangle

If I don't deal with my interior drama what will happen? In time your interior Drama Triangle made up of thoughts and feelings of persecution, victimization, and self-rescuing, will poison your love relationships. You'll mess up your relationships with your kids. You'll blow it with those you are trying to help. This is how true love and soul mates turn into true disaster and soul hates.

How do I keep this from happening? You may become a good student of cognitive-behavioral therapy and learn to recognize and stop cognitive distortions, because you know that how you think determines how you feel. If you are a good meditator you will learn to observe your thoughts, and therefore disassociate from your mental tendency to persecute, victimize, or rescue yourself. The result is that you will be less anxious and less depressed. You won't jump into the Drama Triangle so much or so easily. These are major improvements. You cannot have peace of mind and be in the Drama Triangle at the same time. When you get it out of your relationships and your thoughts you are much more likely to experience peace of mind.

How do my dreams affect my ability to get out of the Drama Triangle? Let's say you work hard at getting out of the Drama Triangle in your relationships. You recognize that you will always fall back into it if you don't get out of it in your thinking as well, so you work hard at that. But what about your dreams? What about that two and a half hours every night, spread out over the eight hours that you are sleeping, when you relapse into drama? This is the reason why most

5: How the Drama Triangle Shows Up in The Three Realms

therapy doesn't stick. You go home and regress into replaying old home videos on your internal DVD player all night in your dreams. It starts with the dream incubation that you do as you are falling asleep, as you go to sleep worried or numbing yourself our, lost in some TV show or video. Then in your dreams the soap operas start. Your old home videos produce dramas that validate why you should continue to feel the way you did when you were six and why you should continue to function with the world view you had Way Back When. The work you did at that therapy session gets undone. The accomplishments and successes of the day get reframed in terms of your childhood insecurity and your innate narcissism. Take a look at a cross-section of your dreams, focusing on the emotions you feel during your dreams and the conclusions that you end up drawing within them. Do you tend to regress into the drama of your childhood cultural scripting when you are dreaming?

Why are dreams generally regressive when seen from our normal waking perspective? While dreaming itself is supportive, important, and anything but regressive, the perspective from which we view them determines whether or not they manufacture drama. Unless there is some process of reframing what is going on in dreams, the Drama Triangle is reinforced while your are dreaming. It then has undesirable effects on your waking emotions, thinking, and relationships.

Don't my dreams stop having an effect when I forget them? No. They reverberate throughout your consciousness by setting an emotional tone, a perceptual reality, and an approach to cognitive problem solving that limits you in what you see and experience in your waking life. *The drama in your dreams keeps you dreaming and asleep in your waking life.* Therapy is undone; you wake up feeling not so super without knowing why; reactivity is reinforced; a bias toward seeing the world in the same old not-so-creative-way is reinforced. This is because of how our waking identity normally interprets dream events and the emotional and cognitive conclusions it draws from them while we are dreaming. It is not because dreams are inherently regressive. They are not.

How do we know that dreams are not regressive? When you take the perspective of other characters in the dream you will discover that most of them are not supportive of drama, or of your regressive perceptions and conclusions about the dream and its meaning. On the contrary, most personify *emerging potentials* that are more awake, alive, balanced, detached, free, and clear than you are. Consequently, they serve as good role models, and their advice is not to be dismissed out of hand.

So why not just pray? Why not just meditate? Why not just think happy thoughts? Why not just keep doing what you do – work at being a good, helpful person who takes care of the responsibilities on your plate today? Use whatever tools work for you. Emphasize tools that incrementally, developmentally, wake you up in an authentic way from within, that avoid the roller coaster and speed up the development of your selectivity regarding drama. That is the major criteria to consider which tool to use: "How effective is it at waking me up out of the Drama Triangle in the three realms today?"

How important is it to surround myself with perspectives that are relatively out of the Drama Triangle? Doing so is extremely effective. This is a major reason why people join monasteries and form spiritually-based groups. While it is both important and necessary to surround yourself with those who are relatively out of Drama in your waking world, it is insufficient. You need to surround yourself with such perspectives in your internal spaces as well or you will project your interior confusion and misperceptions onto the people and events of the external world.

How do I keep from doing so? When you interview the personifications of your life issues and your dream characters you will generally find you are dealing with authentic perspectives that are relatively out of Drama. The key here is *authentic*. The dream characters you interview are intrinsic to your own life compass and express your own emerging potentials, regardless of where you are on your developmental path. No one has to convince you of this; you will be able to evaluate it for yourself when you do IDL interviewing.

How is waking life like dreaming? Waking life is by nature like a dramatic dream in which you are attempting to awaken. The goal is not to stop dreaming, but to be lucid in that life dream. It is not enough to just wake up within it, because that means to colonize the dreaming state with the stunted level of your current waking development. When you become lucid in dreams and change or manipulate the dream, instead of waking up by listening to and learning from the dream drama, you merely export your waking biases and misperceptions into the dreamscape, conquering it and manipulating it. This is the basic problem with most approaches to lucid dreaming.

What are some of the uses of lucid dreaming? Among the many legitimate uses for dream lucidity is using them to develop confidence in dealing with fears, to practice life skills in the fail-safe circumstance of a death-free dream reality and to create healing possibilities that do not exist in waking life. Still more important is to learn to interview other characters in your dreams while you are dreaming in order to benefit from their perspective. With lucid dreaming we infuse the dream with greater self-awareness, which is good if our self-awareness is evolved enough to listen rather than merely control. However, this is generally not the case. For most of us, the self that wakes up in a dream is itself sleepwalking through life. That "awake" self is itself developmentally arrested. It's like putting a drunk behind the steering wheel of a car.

Can I learn to meditate in my dreams? Yes. More important than lucid dreaming is learning to meditate in your dreams. Awareness is the core of consciousness as opposed to unconsciousness. Consciousness, as wakefulness, is awareness aware of itself. Unconsciousness, as deep sleep, is awareness unaware of itself. Anything that cultivates the witness, where you develop objectivity, learning to watch yourself immersed in the drama of your relationships, your life, your thoughts, your feelings, and your dreams – is good. Meditation and the assimilation of perspectives of those people and interviewed emerging potentials that are relatively objective are all important in this respect.

What is "luminosity?" What you will also accomplish, at the same time, is the infusion of your life dream with greater luminosity. Luminosity is the core of deep sleep, of unconsciousness. It is formless, high causal and non-dual empty, open, all-inclusive state of pure awareness that is always already present. Metaphorically, it is interstellar space, where there is no language, space, or time, because there are no dualities by which to generate such distinctions.

People usually associate all-inclusive pure awareness with beingness, God, consciousness, or pure consciousness. This is mistaken, muddy thinking that results in a misperception of the real potential of what it means to wake up into luminosity. This is why Buddhism makes consciousness itself, or pure beingness, one of the five interdependent conditions that create identity. The other four are senses, feelings, thoughts, and images. In Buddhism, apart from the interaction of these five, there is no self. There is no identity. This deep sleep and deep space like luminosity is the plenum out of which all consciousness, beingness, and divinity arises. It is the source of creativity, not creativity itself. It is the source of the organizational matrices that generated the Big Bang. It is the nothingness beyond the oppositions of something and nothing. Luminosity is an excellent word for a space that is brimming with emerging potentials, wanting, waiting to be born. That is what negentropy, life, and evolution is all about. It isn't about us any more than we are about our hands or our feet or our words. These are mere tools for the manifestation of whatever that is wanting to come into expression.

How do I increase luminosity? You want to infuse the dream of your waking life with this luminosity at the same time that you are infusing it with greater self-awareness. This integrates both heightened wakefulness and heightened "deep sleep" into the dream state of normal life. When you do so, you developmentally awaken in a balanced way. The dream of life becomes gradually a sacred game, not to be taken overly seriously, but handled with compassion, wisdom, confidence, acceptance, inner peace, and objectivity, core qualities that can be associated with the round of every breath. Life becomes humorous, not in a trivial way, but in your own tendency to take yourself, others, and the drama of life seriously. You see that and instead of reacting, you smile about it. It's a humor that is cosmic, because it laughs at itself. This sets you up to be naturally inoculated against Drama on all levels while enjoying the preciousness of the slow, gradual developmental pace of natural unfolding, rather than always trying to push the river out of some deep down fear that you may be wrong – that there really might not be a God, a soul, a life after death, cosmic justice or a cosmic plan. When you can live happily without rescuing yourself with such comfortable metaphysical assumptions that have little to do with reality, you are moving beyond your fear of death, of non-existence, and the frantic search for a savior, god, or spiritual practice to rescue you.

How are we our own worst enemies? All of us are trying to become more awake. However, we are our own worst enemies, primarily because of the way we generate Drama in our relationships, thoughts, feelings, and dreams. We enjoy life more, find inner peace, and wake up more when we identify when we are in Drama in any of these realms and opt out. Simply choosing not to play is good enough. How others respond to that (generally with discomfort because they have to adjust to a different you), is, in all compassion, not your concern. Just tell them that you are trying to learn to stay out of the Drama Triangle and ask for their help. Explain to them what it is and ask them to tell you when they see you playing the rescuer, victim, or persecutor. This will educate them and encourage them to buy into the radical shift in culture that you are attempting to bring about for yourself in your world.

6: Love and the Drama Triangle

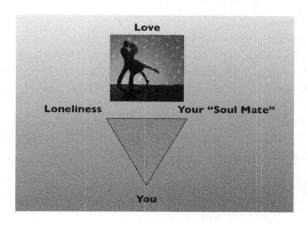

The Greeks had a tripartite concept of love. *Eros,* which is biological and intensely emotional, tends to peak early, be highly addictive and crash suddenly, leaving one depressed, confused and alone. It represents a temporary *state* of consciousness. You can also get into an eros relationship with a sport, hobby or addiction. *Philos* is the love between friends and is based on common interests, like work, raising children, music, football, drinking, eating, watching movies and laughing together. *Philos* is more sustainable than eros and may be deep or shallow, depending on the depth and breadth of shared interests. It represents mutual interests based on shared aptitudes, or *lines* of development. *Agape* is not love for one another, but a shared love for a common direction in life. The depth and breadth of this shared direction determines the sustainability of *agape.* For instance, many couples stay together to raise children. What happens to the relationship when the children are grown? It may end, mellow into a friendship or find some other common goal. Genuine *agape* involves mutual support in advancing *stages* of development. The two people do not need to be on the same developmental level, only bound by a mutual desire to support the other in self-actualization. All three of these forms of love are important and support growth when balanced with the others.

Is there a type of love that is less susceptible to the Drama Triangle? Yes. With agape you are less susceptible. However, regardless of the type of love you experience, you remain susceptible to the Drama Triangle. You know what *eros* within the Drama Triangle looks and feels like. It is an intense emotional game of passion that often also includes insecurity, possessiveness, disappointment, betrayal and revenge. Most love songs and romance novels are about eros and the Drama Triangle. The better question is, "Can one do *eros* outside of the Drama

6: Love and the Drama Triangle

Triangle?" The answer is, "Yes, of course, but it's not easy." Those who think they can are generally naive. *Philos* naturally involves less drama, but friends tend to validate each other in their stuckness and play similar, supporting roles in the Drama Triangle. These "friends" validate your addictions by sharing your views on who to love and who to hate. They are unlikely to challenge your addictions or your life decisions. They tend to feel victimized in the same ways that you do and rescue the same sorts of people that you do. In short, friends tend to be stuck pretty much where you're stuck.

Of course, a "real" friend challenges your stuckness and helps you to grow, whether you like it or not. A classical example of such a friend would be Socrates, who made everyone question all their assumptions about what was true and good, and was generally considered a pain in the ass. Few of us choose to surround ourselves with such friends, because they irritate us and make us uncomfortable. Of these three types of love, *agape* is the most detached and abstracted from drama. There is little personalization of the relationship and, therefore, less likelihood that you will feel hurt by your unmet expectations. Clearly, you need all three types of love. If you settle for *eros,* you may well miss out on *philos* and *agape*. If you settle for *eros* and *philos,* you may well miss out on *agape*. If you insist on *agape,* it is possible that you may also achieve *philos* and *eros,* but there is no guarantee. To the extent that you define love as intimate and honest, you can't have it and the Drama Triangle, too. You have to decide which is more important to you: drama or love. If you decide on love, recognize that people who do drama are likely to select themselves out of your life, because you won't play. You may experience this as loneliness. Consider the possibility that you don't need to feel lonely. You are making space in your life for quality, non-dramatic relationships to form.

How good a job do you do at staying out of the Drama Triangle in your love relationships? What do you think would need to change for you to do a better job at that?

Soul Mates – Eternal Love?

What makes the idea of Soul Mates so attractive? The idea that there is one other special person who is a perfect fit for you is very attractive. It allows you to feel the specialness and uniqueness of your love and the sacredness of the bond you have with the one you love. It proclaims to the world and to yourself that this is the One for You, the right, timeless, and everlasting Love of Your Life. As a result, you give yourself permission to commit yourself completely and wholly to this person, because they are your perfect match. Any problems, any misunderstandings, will melt into insignificance within the mutual knowledge that this is a love that lasts forever.

6: Love and the Drama Triangle

The idea of Soul Mates takes the ideal of Courtly Love, developed during the Middle Ages when knights fought to win the favor of some fair lady, to a new, higher level. The romantic ideal of love was refined in the genre of romantic novels, beginning with the works of Jane Austin, until it attained an exalted metaphysical pinnacle as the concept of Soul Mate, in which the bond of love is created and sanctioned by God, *karma, dharma* and an eternal Divine Order. Seen in such a light, anything that stands between you and your Soul Mate becomes a sin against Nature, Reality, Love, and Truth.

What human needs does a belief in Soul Mates fulfill? Clearly, a belief in Soul Mates meets the needs of many people. What are those needs? People need to feel special, and the idea of Soul Mates makes people feel special. People need to have their relationship choices validated so that they don't have to question their judgment, because that would get in the way of abandoning themselves completely to the unique specialness of their love. In addition, contemplating the consequences of a poor choice gets in the way of the dizzying reality of the moment and the possibilities for future happiness it portends. Why not trust in the Power of Love? It feels beautiful, true, and right. Does it not show disrespect not to trust such a sacred thing?

What is the relationship between the concept of Soul Mates and the Drama Triangle? If this sounds like the Drama Triangle, it's because it is. The Drama Triangle is a psychological game played between people, as well as in your thoughts and in your dreams. It consists of three roles, Persecutor, Victim, and Rescuer. When you play one role you eventually end up playing the other two. It's unavoidable. Soul Mates are Rescuers in the Drama Triangle.

Are Soul Mates always lovers? No. Gurus are a special variety of Soul Mate. Both lovers and Gurus come into your life to rescue you from loneliness, boredom, and insecurity, to show you the way to happiness, bliss and enlightenment. They give your life meaning it didn't have before. What's wrong with that? The problem is that you have fallen in love with your own idealization that you want and think you need. You are ignoring who the other person really is, because that's not who you need them to be. You want and need them to be your rescuer.

But rescuers have a nasty habit of turning into persecutors. How come? At some point your Soul Mate's behavior will be seen to no longer live up to your unrealistic, idealistic expectations for them. What Guru does not also fit this description? When this happens it is often experienced as rejection or abandonment. You may try many different means to get them to change, to become the person you know that they "really" are. But your well-meaning efforts will be experienced as non-acceptance and met with resistance. Prince Charming has turned into a frog or even worse, a warty toad.

What are some other ways that believing in Soul Mates rescues us within the

6: Love and the Drama Triangle

Drama Triangle? Your Soul Mate is there to rescue you from all sorts of Persecutors: boredom, loneliness, and fear of having made a poor choice, while rescuing you *to* other desirable things: elevated mood, a sense of sacredness in relationship, happiness, excitement, security and prosperity.

The idea of Soul Mates not only makes you feel special; it validates your choice of partners. It has the additional advantage of justifying bad choices. When the relationship crashes, you can tell yourself that while this was a Match Made in Heaven, it wasn't "meant to be" at this time. You are able to maintain both your belief in Soul Mates and the rightness of your choice of a disastrous match. The relationship failed not because you both were in the Drama Triangle but because of "fate." Fate, however, is another way of expressing a belief in our own powerlessness, of our own Victim status within the Drama Triangle, is it not?

This is also the thinking when your Soul Mate is already in a committed relationship. This complication does not change the fact that the relationship was Meant to Be and that Love Will Find a Way. It's karma, destiny, and fate that you have found each other over all these centuries, out of all these millions of people; somehow life will change so that you will be able to be together to put the universe into the harmony, order, beauty, truth, and love that was Meant to Be. In the presence of such timeless, sacred love, how meaningful are the social vows of marriage? People do not understand the power and preeminence of Real, Divine Love.

Such thinking shows the addictive power of rescuing within the Drama Triangle to summon up any and all rationalizations to justify drama. How is it different than an alcoholic or cocaine addict justifying using just this once?

How about multiple Soul Mates? What about when you are sure someone is your Soul Mate but then another person comes along and you are even more sure this new one is your Soul Mate? You were mistaken before, but *now* you are sure. You *know* this one is *really* your soul mate. How do you know? It feels right; you've never felt like this; there is a powerful, spiritual energy not just from one but from several of your chakras to this other person. When you ask them about it, they feel it too. That's proof. It couldn't be that they are just saying what you want to hear so they can get what they want from you. It couldn't be that they feel it too but that the feeling works to validate what they feel and what they want. No; it's nothing like that.

Belief in Soul Mates is harmless and gives my life meaning! Why spoil the fun? Alas. When a belief is convenient, self-validating, and justifies doing whatever you already want to do, it is wise to take a peek behind the curtain. Is the Great and Powerful Oz really Great and Powerful, or is he a petty carnival operator making money out of generating mass delusion? Asking such a question smacks of cynicism and disrespect. Isn't it cruel, like taking candy from a child? What harm is the candy? Why can't one just leave well enough alone? Even if a belief in Soul Mates is a delusion, it is harmless, is it not? Why not just let lovers in love be? Why spoil the fun? Why not just let people find out on their own?

What if a baby has a cigarette instead of candy? There are cases of two year olds becoming addicted to cigarettes or alcohol because their parents think it is "cute." Like cigarettes and alcohol, the concept of Soul Mates is addictive. How else does one explain how effectively it has taken root in the popular imagination? How else does one explain why it has remained viable in some segments of culture for decades?

The problem with viewing Soul Mates as an understandable and harmless belief is that it allows you to stand by while lives are wrecked and children are raised in unnecessary adversity. Is it harmless if your daughter has children with her Soul Mate, who turns out to be an alcoholic, gambler, and child molester? What are the consequences for your daughter? What are the consequences for your grandchildren? Are those consequences all in Divine Order? Do you want to spend years of your life worrying about the welfare of your own grandchildren, who are being raised in circumstances that are abusive, but that you can do little to change?

Why do we continue to tell ourselves, "This time is different?" Because landing in misery in the Drama Triangle is so highly predictable it is amazing that most people manage to fool themselves into thinking that *this time*, with *this person*, things will be different. If you like living in the Drama Triangle, you'll love believing in Soul Mates. You'll love trading in last year's model Guru for the new, improved, highly recommended Real and True Guru.

How can I tell if my belief in Soul Mates is helpful? Here some questions to ask yourself. Does a belief in Soul Mates make poor judgment about relationships choices more or less likely? Is a belief in Soul Mates likely to be true – that there is only one right person for you in all the universe and you have found them – or is it more likely that you are indulging in a delusion that validates your current feelings?

The inconvenient truth is that believing in Soul Mates is based on fear. It assumes that abundance does not exist in the universe, that this one lover or teacher that seems so special, so right, is the only source of deep, satisfying, complete love that you will ever find in the universe. Wouldn't such a universe be narrow, petty, and impoverished? It also assumes that you have to settle for what you've got, because better is not going to come around. Is that true? How do you know?

It is hard work finding appropriate partners and spiritual teachers. You'll be disappointed and get rejected. You'll make mistakes and then have to look at why you did so and learn from them. That's difficult. No one likes being confronted with the fact that, despite their best judgment and strong feelings, they were flat-out wrong or just plain foolish in their choice in partners or spiritual teachers. It's much easier to leave the choice to chance, magic, and delusional thinking and just pray that reality won't catch up.

However, once you get the hang of it, it's not so bad being wrong and foolish. I make a point of being wrong and foolish at least six times before breakfast, and then attempt to improve on my failure rate as the day goes on. Pretending you're not stupid, ignorant, and mistaken takes energy away from enjoying life. Why not just admit to yourself and everyone else that you are a hopeless dweeb? They will not only be taken aback by your honesty but pleasantly surprised when you do something minor right, like remember their name. You can then learn from your mistakes instead of hiding them, as if they were bad or wrong. Mistakes are a good thing; they're how you learn.

The truth about Soul Mates is that there is no perfect match for you; there is no perfect teacher, Guru or Master either. Everyone you meet is a fallible human being. The more you get to know your partner the more you will recognize just how confused and stuck they are, just like you. When you give your partner or teacher permission to be imperfect you are giving yourself permission to be imperfect. You no longer have to try to be someone's Soul Mate. Instead you can just be you, which is both more unique and wonderful than any Soul Mate.

If you have an eleven year old child, grandchild, nephew, niece, or friend, why not talk to them about all this? You could save them years of heartbreak. You could save yourself years of protecting children from the disastrous decisions of stupid adults. Why not have them read this and ask them what they think? Help them think these issues through before they get blinded by teenage hormones. Love does not have to be blind. Reason exists to improve love. Objectivity and love not only co-exist, but need each other to make decisions that not only feel good, but stand the test of time.

11: Words that Keep You Stuck in Drama

7: Addiction and the Drama Triangle

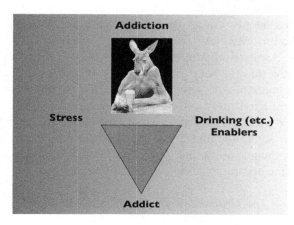

Addictions are wonderful, useful things or you would have gotten rid of yours long ago. As the old joke goes, "If you had to choose between losing weight and giving up chocolate, would you choose milk, bitter, or chocolate with nuts?" It doesn't matter if you are addicted to cigarettes, alcohol, drugs, self-criticism, rages, sex, the internet, coffee, email, gambling, texting, shopping, gossip, exercise, soap operas, shoes or work. All addictions, without exception, occur within the tender embrace of the Drama Triangle. You are an addict, and addicts are the Victim of their persecuting addictions. They live for the next rescuing.

What is the function of my addictions? To rescue you, the Victim, from something or somebody: boredom, anxiety, depression, shyness, the monotony of work, an abusive spouse, yelling, kids, stress. Your addiction will always present itself as your Rescuer. The problem is that it is both the Rescuer and the Persecutor. When you indulge in your addiction, are you not both rescuing and persecuting yourself?

How do I keep myself addicted? Because you like the feeling of being rescued, you play all sorts of games to maintain your favorite addictions. I have known smokers who had "spiritualized" the smoke so that it was no longer harmful; I have known tantra sexual practitioners who had so spiritualized sex that they were no longer in the Drama Triangle about it. This is the nature of addiction; you tell yourself that you aren't really addicted or that even if you are, it's not that big a problem. You tell yourself that you can control it; you only need to cut down. You tell yourself that because you are out of the Drama Triangle, you can do your addiction without it being an addiction. You have evolved beyond that.

Is my basic problem my addiction? The problem, at least in most cases, is not your addiction; it's that your addiction keeps you a prisoner of the Drama Triangle. Can you do your addiction, just a little, and be out of the Drama

Triangle? How do you know if you are fooling yourself of not? The recommended default position recommended by IDL is to assume that you are fooling yourself, that you are indeed deeply asleep, dreaming and sleepwalking through your life, lost within the Drama Triangle.

What are your favorite addictions? How do they rescue you? How do they persecute you? How do they keep you in the role of the Victim? Are you ready to face the fact that you can't do your favorite addictions and be out of the Drama Triangle, or do you need more failure and misery first? If so, how much more? Six months? Three years? Ten years? The point is to take your focus off hating yourself for your addiction and focus on breaking the core addiction that is beneath all your others: your addiction to the Drama Triangle. Get out of it and you may develop the common sense to take care of yourself.

The Drama Triangle is Highly Addictive

What is the relationship between the Drama Triangle and addiction? The Drama Triangle helps to explain why we do most of the things that we do. We follow the latest and greatest spiritual fad, fight with our families, go to work, and go bankrupt all within the Drama Triangle. Getting married, divorced, or taking a job are often forms of self-rescuing. We may do some of these things, like work, clean up or have sex, to escape the persecution of someone or some condition. All of these activities tend to become ingrained habits or self-sustaining addictions; we all know that breaking free of them is no easy task.

Is the Drama Triangle all bad? A lot of good, some would argue most or all of the good, that happens in the world happens within the Drama Triangle. An analogy would be that ill-gotten fortunes get passed on to people who may do less exploitative things with that money. Therefore, rather than imagining that the Drama Triangle is a bad thing, it is better to think of it as a condition that produces unnecessary misery for us and for those around us while impeding our ability to problem solve and reach our goals.

Is the Drama Triangle the major source of our misery and suffering? Certainly the Drama Triangle is hardly the only motivator for all of these different pursuits and it is conceivable that all of them can be done outside the Drama Triangle. However, once you understand how the Drama Triangle works, you will see it everywhere you look, including in your own dreams. It is a fundamental way that people sabotage their happiness. If you learn to recognize and eliminate it in the three realms of relationships, thinking, and dreaming you will have removed a major barrier to your growth. This is a skill IDL teaches its students.

How is freedom from the Drama Triangle related to waking up, lucidity and enlightenment? If we want to wake up we need to break our addiction to the Drama Triangle, which is different from drama itself. Drama is the normal predicament of life. We get victimized. We need rescuing sometimes. Persecution is real. However, just because we get victimized that does not mean we are forced to play the unhealthy role of *Victim*. That's our choice. Because we sometimes need rescuing from disease, fires, floods, and bad governments, that doesn't mean that we are wise to get into the role of rescuer. We aren't, because the role of rescuer is sick and when we are in it we get sick. It makes us sick. Because persecution is real it does not follow that it is healthy to persecute either others or ourselves. That is abusive, and abuse is dysfunctional. Drama is a fact of life; the Drama Triangle is a choice. You don't have to go there, and you won't if you are wise. Waking up out of the Drama Triangle is a core definition of what it means to wake up. This is because the Drama Triangle is a functional definition of karma, *dukkha*, illusion, maya, and the suffering that delusion creates. The distinction between drama and Drama has to be made before we can learn to surf through the dramas of life without having them overwhelm us and drown us.

Can I play one role, like Rescuer, and avoid playing the others, like Victim? No. If you play one role in the Drama Triangle you will end up playing them all. If you become a professional rescuer (doctor, cop, social worker, etc.) and give more than you get, you burn out sooner or later. If you persecute others (always for their own good) you are persecuting those parts of yourself that they represent. If you play the Victim you are saying you are powerless. You are giving your power to people and circumstances that you do not like or respect. Is it wise to do that?

Is the Drama Triangle a perpetual roller coaster? Yes. Another problem is that like addictions, these roles put us into temporary *states*. We get temporary relief by blasting someone else with the sword of righteous indignation and knowing that we are telling them the truth. We are more interested in being right than being loving. We get temporary relief from the abuses and abusers of the world by going passive, hunkering down, retreating into hopelessness, helplessness, and powerlessness, playing the victim. We get to experience the power of whining and blaming. Wonderful! Perhaps we get a sense of usefulness and meaningfulness out of rescuing others.

Are Rescuers addicted to their opinions? Generally, yes. Rescuers don't need to ask; they already know what needs to be done. They may ask questions, use the answers to validate their preconceptions, and interpose their formulaic diagnosis and treatment: ("You're bipolar; you need meds;" "Your economy is sick, you need privatization, elimination of trade barriers, reduction of government services, and austerity." "You need to behave." "You need to make good grades.")

Are public servants socially-sanctioned Helpers? Yes. The role of cop or fireman is not inherently a rescuer, because they function under a social contract that gives them permission to break down your door and hose the interior of your home, or put you in jail. Of course that doesn't mean that what they do and how they do it doesn't typically reek of Drama. It does.

Why isn't rescuing helping? When you "hurt my feelings" I am putting you in the role of Persecutor and myself in the role of Victim. Typically, I respond within the context of the Drama Triangle. I go passive and feel hurt by playing the Victim, or counter-attack by playing the Persecutor, or attempt to rescue you, me, or our relationship by explaining or changing the subject. For instance I might attempt to rescue you by returning injury with love, like good Christians, Moslems, Jews, and Hindus are taught to do, or I might attempt to rescue you by explaining to you how you are either mistaken or don't see the entire picture. I might attempt to rescue myself by avoiding you, by calling a friend and having a sob fest, by losing myself in a book or good movie, by getting something to eat (always a great option), or by simply going to sleep. I might attempt to rescue the relationship by changing the subject or refocusing on areas of mutual agreement. None of these strategies stop the Drama because the "solutions" are all substitutions of one role for another. You stay in the Drama Triangle; you've just changed roles. However of the three realms of the Drama Triangle, working on stopping dysfunctional drama in relationships is relatively easy and highly productive. It will carve out peace in your life where there was none before and set the context for success at tackling the other two realms.

Is it not enough to break my addiction to the Drama Triangle in my relationships? No. If I do manage to not fall into any of those three roles with you, does that mean that I am staying out of them in my own head? Not necessarily. I may still be persecuting myself with all sorts of obviously true statements of how incompetent, inefficient, unloving, I am. If I am persecuting myself with such thoughts and feelings, then I will also be in the role of Victim, since I will be making myself feel helpless and hopeless. At the same time I may be constantly figuring out what to do or think to rescue myself from this self-persecution. Most people spend most of their waking hours in all three of these roles. They live their lives in the context of the Drama Triangle. Indeed, they can't even imagine what life would be like outside it. Can you? Do you have an inner life outside of the Drama Triangle? If you closely examine your thoughts and feelings, you will probably conclude, as I have, that for the most part, you do not.

8: Getting Out of the Drama Triangle

Are there any alternatives to the Drama Triangle? Yes. Anything and everything is potentially an alternative to the Drama Triangle because it is not about what you do but the consciousness or world view in which you do it. There is a real difference between victimization and being a victim, between being a helper and being a rescuer, and between being assertive and being a persecutor. Are there some guidelines or ways to know when you are out of the Drama Triangle? Yes.

How do we speed our escape from our own personal Drama Triangle? It is not easy for any of us to objectify the Drama Triangle, to get to the place where we realize that all along we have had what we have been searching for. The answer lies in understanding the toxicity of these roles and moving to a neutral place in relation to them. This place can be called taking on the role of a "Helper."

Are Helpers out of the Drama Triangle? No. Helpers are only relatively out of the Drama Triangle. In relationship to the current Drama Triangle you develop objectivity, but this objectivity is only relative. In the context of some broader context, you remain in the Drama Triangle and do not realize it because you are subjectively enmeshed, as you normally are in your dreams. However, this is not so important, because what matters is to wake up out of those instances of the Drama Triangle that relate to your present life misery and suffering, not some future level which you may or may not ever attain.

How important is freedom from the Drama Triangle in relationship to states of wakefulness like lucid dreaming or meditation? Similarly, learning to lucid dream is trivial in importance in relationship to learning to wake up out of the Drama Triangle in the three realms. Again, this is because you can lucid dream all the time and stay stuck at your current level of development. However, IDL demonstrates that to the extent that you wake up out of the Drama Triangle in all

8: Getting Out of the Drama Triangle

three realms you cut chains that are holding back your development; you will naturally and smoothly rise to a broader, more inclusive perspective as you do so, regardless of your level of development. This applies to committed meditators as well, as there is no necessary relationship between meditation and freedom from the Drama Triangle. While meditation definitely supports detachment and objectivity associated with freedom from the Drama Triangle, IDL focuses on helping you identify when and how you are stuck in the three roles in all three realms. The result is that you can identify when and how you are stuck so that you have a choice. Awareness is key; if you are unaware of how you are stuck you are highly unlikely to become unstuck, regardless of how much you meditate.

What is lucidity in relationship to the Drama Triangle? As a Helper, you become pellucid toward your life. Pellucidity is being awake to your dramas without attempting to manipulate, change, or control them, rather like the sky embraces clouds, thunderstorms, and tornadoes with equal equanimity. You simply accept what occurs and respect events and people for what they are.

What this looks like in a dream is that you are lucid in the sense that you recognize invitations to drama but to not accept them. Instead, you remain lucid in relationship to them, in a space where you honor the monster, the threat, the desire to rescue or to blame and witness it without judgment. This puts you in a place of clarity regarding decision-making. You can ask for more information and respond in a way that honors the needs of all concerned. This is indeed a transformational definition of lucidity.

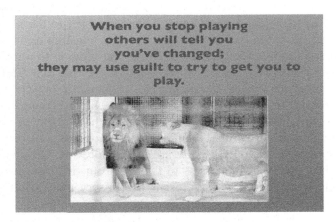

How do I know if I am relatively out of the Drama Triangle? You will ask if you can help instead of assuming that your help is needed. You will stop and check to see if your contributions are indeed helpful, effective, and appreciated. You will stop and wait for a request for additional assistance instead of

8: Getting Out of the Drama Triangle

automatically assuming that your contributions are needed. Exceptions are civically sanctioned Rescuers, such as nurses, police, and firemen. These people have given contractual prior permission to break open doors, hose down possessions, rip clothes off people and use force if necessary. You will be relatively detached because you have cultivated the witness relative to your own particular life Drama Triangles.

What are some of the other signs of being in the role of Helper? When you take roles in life, such as worker, caretaker or even consumer, and you choose to do so in order to serve all sentient beings, you are much more likely to be relatively out of the Drama Triangle in the Helper position. We have seen that in Buddhism this approach is called *upaya*, or "cunning benevolence." Avatars and Bodhisattvas, in the proper understanding of these roles, are not Rescuers but divine helpers. You do not have to attain such exalted status to move into the perspective of Helper. Helpers also manifest a balance of characteristics that are an antidote to each of the three roles of the Drama Triangle. These can be summarized as wisdom, the antidote to persecution, inner peace, the antidote to victimhood, and empathy, the antidote to rescuing.

Is it wise to assume I am always in the Drama Triangle? Yes. This will keep you from presuming that you are out of the delusion when you are not. Ask yourself throughout your day, "If I were in the Drama Triangle now, what role would I be in?" Look for examples in your world and in your thoughts. For example, what is the last thing you ate? Why did you eat that instead of something else? Because it was handy? Because you liked it? Of course! However, try asking another sort of question: "If I was eating that to rescue myself from some sense of persecution in the Drama Triangle, what would it be?" For example, one reason why people gain weight and can't lose it is because they experience hunger as persecuting. Is it? No. The physical sensation of hunger exists outside the Drama Triangle; you get to choose what meaning to project onto those sensations. So, begin by considering that whatever you are doing, moment to moment, may be occurring within the context of the Drama Triangle.

Can there be peace of mind within the Drama Triangle? No. When you view life from within the roles of Victim, Persecutor and Rescuer, you are at war with yourself. Is it any wonder that individuals, nations and religions end up being at war?

What are some other suggestions about getting out of the Drama Triangle? Trust that there really is such a thing as life outside the Drama Triangle. Give yourself permission to get out. Don't give yourself reasons why you can't or won't get out of drama, such as, "Life would be boring." "I would lose all my friends." Such rationalizations and excuses are indications that you want to stay asleep, dreaming and sleepwalking. It also reflects a lack of confidence in the ability of those you love to wake up. If your daily work involves rescuing or

8: Getting Out of the Drama Triangle

persecuting people or feeling like a victim, you may need to find alternatives for becoming more creative in your work.

If someone accuses you of being in the role of the Persecutor, give them the benefit of the doubt. That's because we never see ourselves as persecutors. We know that what we are saying or doing is only for the good of others, but that is a form of grandiosity and mind-reading. We think we have no choice but to defend ourselves against some perceived threat or attack, and so we do not feel that our reactions are persecuting, when they are.

Understand the role of the Helper and how it is different from the role of rescuer.

Know what it feels like and looks like to be out of the Drama Triangle. Refuse to play. Recognize and decline all invitations to play.

Explain the Drama Triangle to your family and friends. Ask them to tell you when you are in one or another of the three roles.

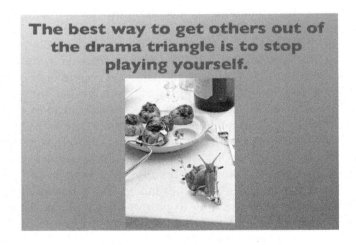

Understand the antithesis to these three roles, the Socratic Triune.

9: Using the Empowerment Dynamic

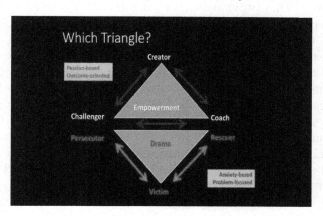

David Emerald has developed an alternative to the Drama Triangle which he calls the "empowerment dynamic." It involves the substitution of the roles of Persecutor, Victim and Rescuer with healthy alternatives which are accompanied with rational thoughts that substitute for the cognitive distortions that support the roles of the Drama Triangle. These healthy roles and thoughts produce positive emotions and behaviors and can be thought of as three manifestations of the role of Helper. Instead of fear-based action they generate behaviors that are motivated by creative passion. Ideally, the empowerment dynamic generates behavior that is solution-focused in relationship to the problem-focused behavior of action within the Drama Triangle.

How does the role of "Challenger" serve as an antidote to the role of Persecutor? According to The Empowerment Dynamic, the Persecutor evolves into the "Challenger" who thinks, "You can do it!" They see all of life's challenges as opportunities for growth. Challengers ask themselves, "What is my intention?" instead of assuming they know what is best or right. Instead of putting others or themselves down they build up and gather new, helpful information. They recognize and speak to the potentials in others, often unrecognized. Challengers produce clear structures and guidelines for accomplishment. They challenge by asking, "What do you want to do?" "Who do you want to become?" "What are you committed to?" "You aren't doing what you said you were going to do; what are you going to do about it?" They think, "I can hold others to a high standard because I see the best in them, and I can do it in a way that is kind, thoughtful and empowering."

Challengers state boundaries such as, "We are agreeing not to interrupt or change the subject." Challengers listen without personalizing; they do not take on the problems of others and make them their problems. Challengers make expectations clear: "I want you to keep your agreement. Please have it done by our next meeting." They provide choices: "If you cannot keep an appointment you can call to reschedule with 24 hours notice or you can pay me for the missed appointment." Challengers generate feelings of security, respect and trust and behaviors that are responsible and clear. They call forth learning and growth while provoking and evoking conscious and constructive action.

How does the role of "Evolver" serve as an antidote to the role of Victim? The Victim evolves into the "Creator" in Emerald's system, a role that is also an "achiever" or "evolver" who thinks, "I can do it!" "I am capable!" Evolvers state what they want, create a plan, follow it and take action to achieve their goals. They keep their agreements, which means they also learn not to over-commit. Evolvers ask themselves, "What do I want and what do I need?" "How can I get what I need in a healthy way?" "How can I move from reacting to responding?" They think, "I am moving ahead in my life." "This is what I've learned." "I can make my own decisions and create a life I desire for myself." "I can hold myself to a high standard without being critical and pressuring, perfectionistic, or thinking that makes me better than others." Evolvers remember what they have to be thankful for and focus on their strengths, not their weaknesses, limitations and failures. Evolvers ask for help from coaches, not rescuers, meaning that they not only know the difference but recognize that rescuing will only keep them stuck. This generates feelings of empowerment and behaviors that are satisfying because they move Evolvers one step closer to their goals. Evolvers own their power to choose and respond rather than react. They focus on outcomes and solutions rather than on problems.

How does the role of "Coach" serve as an antidote to the role of Rescuer? The Rescuer evolves into the "Coach" who says, "I care about you and I know that you are capable." They ask themselves, "How am I seeing this other person, as a victim or evolver?" Coaches don't do for another person what they can do for themselves. This is not a failure of generosity but rather a statement of confidence in the ability of the other to think, figure things out and take action. Coaches say, "I know you can do this." "What are your next steps?" "What do you need in order to achieve them?" Coaches support and assist, facilitating the development of clarity by asking questions, and asking, "How will you do it?" They provide choices while focusing on solutions rather than problems. This generates feelings of confidence and behaviors that are effective and successful.

IDL views Emerald's system as aspirational. Imagining healthy antidotes to the three roles of the Drama Triangle and exploring ways that you can move into those roles is a form of behavioral substitution that roughly parallels the substitution of healthy, rational statements for cognitive distortions. IDL encourages such substitutions while noting that these positive role descriptions are considerably different from the perspectives of interviewed dream characters and personifications of life issues that are out of the Drama Triangle. The difference is between consciously chosen alternatives to the Drama Triangle and alternatives that are innate and emerging as *experiential* substitutes for specific instances of drama. For IDL, both are needed, with the goal of aligning waking antidotes to the Drama Triangle, such as Emerald's descriptions, with the perspectives of interviewed emerging potentials.

By doing so, all three of these transformed, constructive roles combine into an identity that becomes increasingly transparent. Life becomes less and less about you and your interests and increasingly about what life wants. It involves how you can help yourself and others get out of the way so that life itself can evolve as it moves into a fuller expression of its own infinite potentials.

10: Ways Feelings Keep You Stuck in Drama

Do you recognize who is in this picture? That's Smeagol in his pre-Gollum days, when he just found the One Ring in Tolkein's *Lord of the Rings*.

Is he joyful and happy? You bet!

While there is nothing wrong with emotions in and of themselves, they are a common and powerful way most people keep themselves stuck in the Drama Triangle.

Fear

Fear is generally viewed as a persecuting emotion. Except for horror movies and its use as a weapon to intimidate others, most people want to avoid it. If you are like most people, you will first try to avoid your fear; if that doesn't work, you will fight it; if that still is ineffective, you will get even more scared. These are the strategies that nations as well as individuals tend to use. They ignore problems like failing dams and non-earthquake-proof buildings, hoping that they will go away. If that doesn't work there may be a period of fighting the fear by repairing infrastructure and buildings. But if that doesn't work, such as in war, which may create conditions where one cannot escape from fear, people get even more scared, moving entire populations toward a PTSD-like existence.

When you feel persecuted by some fear do you experience yourself as a Victim? If you do, you experience yourself as powerless and helpless, leading you to then seek rescuing, something or someone to make your fear go away. Because only some 5-10% of all fears are real, almost all experiences of Persecution associated with it are self-generated, due to some misperception of some situation or individual. You are therefore usually seeking a cure for a problem that doesn't exist. For example, if you view strangers as threats you are largely scaring yourself, just as you do when you assume a dream monster or fire can hurt you.

If you then seek rescuing, perhaps by staying at home or by repressing your dreams, are you not marrying yourself to the problems inherent in your Rescuer? In the case of staying at home, you are cutting yourself off from your environment and the many ways it can enrich your life; in the case of your dreams, you are ignoring a major source of contact with creativity and your life compass. Other problems associated with common Rescuers include alcoholism, failed relationships, the escapism of a vacation and increase risk of both accidents and illness. The problems of your "Rescuers" may in time be experienced as Persecutors that in reality loom larger than you imagined your fear to be.

You get to choose whether you experience fear as a persecuting emotion or not. I didn't cure my stage fright until I re-framed my fear as energizing me to do a better job of communication. I didn't overcome the criticalness that was an unrecognized aspect of my self-discipline until I began approaching what I did with loving kindness. When you assume your fear is persecuting you, you guarantee you will view life in a hunkered-down position, from within the Drama Triangle.

IDL recommends that you stop viewing fear as a Persecutor but instead recognize that what is persecuting you are your own thoughts and feelings about your fears. Once this is recognized, your focus can turn to identifying those thoughts you have when your feel afraid. Write them down. Look them over. Are they rational? Generally you will find that you are telling yourself emotionally-based cognitive distortions, statements that *feel* true but are not rational. Once you identify these statements you can learn to identify and substitute more realistic, rational thoughts for them. All of this is explained in *Waking Up*.

When you feel fear you generally experience all three roles of the Drama Triangle. Fear is a Persecutor, you are a Victim, and you feel compelled to Rescue yourself. Do you view fear as a persecuting emotion? When you feel scared or anxious, what do you usually do?

10: Ways Feelings Keep You Stuck in Drama

Anger

When we feel anger it is generally viewed as a rescuing emotion. Why? Because we generally use anger to defend ourselves, to back off a perceived threat. Therefore, when you get angry you probably don't experience yourself in the role of Persecutor. Instead, you feel victimized by some threat, slight or stupidity. Your anger is therefore justified in your mind. Somebody or something has done something to justify you defending yourself from an attack. Anger is your defender, your savior, your Rescuer. When you get angry, aren't you usually rescuing yourself from some fear?

Years ago I used to have fun with this idea with my young daughter. If she would fall down and cry I would bang on the floor and yell, "Bad floor!" If I did something she didn't like I would put out my hand, slap it with the other hand and say, "Bad Daddy!" She would look at me and laugh. I was teaching her how silly it is to project our sense of victimization out onto the world or onto others. Creativity can transform much drama and address it directly.

However, when people are angry at *us*, anger is generally experienced as a persecuting emotion. Anger means we are being attacked, and so, unless we have learned otherwise, we roll automatically into some sort of defensive response.

In both cases, these conclusions are often incorrect. If someone is not attacking you and you only *think* that they are your anger is misplaced, unnecessary, and abusive. You put yourself unnecessarily in the role of Persecutor in the eyes of the other person. If the anger of the other person is not about you but is instead a reaction to their *own* fear, then you only create a problem where none exists by reacting with defensiveness.

When you feel anger you generally experience all three roles of the Drama Triangle. Anger is a Rescuer, you are a Victim of the consequences of your anger, and your anger at yourself or others turns you into a Persecutor.

Your first line of defense is to ask a question to gain information and to keep yourself from reacting. Ask innocently, "Are you angry at me?" The answer will generally be something different: "No, I'm hurt," or "I'm just frustrated" or,

10: Ways Feelings Keep You Stuck in Drama

"Sorry! I'm having a bad hair day! It's not about you!" By encouraging self-reflection instead of defending yourself, you are exhibiting and modeling loving kindness. If you are angry at yourself, write out what you are telling yourself. You will most likely find that your thoughts are cognitive distortions that keep you in the Drama Triangle. If so, use the procedure noted above regarding fear.

Sadness and Grief

Sadness and grief are generally viewed as persecuting emotions. When someone you love dies, do you feel helpless and powerless in the face of your grief? When you feel depressed and alone, do you feel helpless and powerless in the face of your sadness? If misfortune strikes in the form of chronic pain or debilitating illness are you more likely to get worn down by the stress and regress into a bitter, reactive, hurt child? People generally feel that they can't help but be sad and take the role of Victim.

While it is not easy to be sad or to experience grief without getting into the role of Victim, it is not inevitable. Just because you feel sadness or grief it does not mean that you are a Victim, although it certainly may feel that way. You get to choose. For example, bad things happen every day to people and you don't feel sad; people die unnecessarily every day and you don't feel grief. Why not? Mostly because they are not important to you; they live somewhere else; you have never met them. So there is no necessity for you to feel sadness and grief when there is loss, and there is no necessity for you to get into the role of Victim. That you and I do so is a function of familiarity and expectation. We know ourselves, so we have a sense of wanting to maintain a continuity of meaning, of caring, of day-to-day activity that has been interrupted. We have strong expectations of how life is supposed to be for us and for those we know, while our expectations are much less strong for those we do not know. You feel sadness and grief because you take the loss *personally;* it is as if you have lost a part of *yourself.*

Even if I have lost a part of yourself, does that require a response of sadness or grief? No, but it is a normal response. Does that sadness or grief require that you put yourself in the role of Victim in the Drama Triangle? No, and to do so only makes it harder for you to get over your sadness and grief.

When you feel sadness or grief you generally experience all three roles of the Drama Triangle. Sadness or grief can cause you to feel you really are a Victim; these feelings feel like they are persecuting you. In a strange way, they are also Rescuers, because they validate the meaning of your loss. Their presence says, "My loss is *real;* that person, pet, body part, home, or relationship was *meaningful!* To not feel grief or sadness is to deny the reality of the meaningfulness of what you have lost. Therefore, grief and sadness are powerful Rescuers from meaninglessness, even as they create withdrawal from a meaningful, full life.

What are the alternatives? The more that you learn to objectify both your feelings and the human predicament the more you will be able to respond with empathy, compassion and loving caring. This does not mean that you ignore or repress your sadness and grief, but it does mean that you reframe them as existing within some broader context that has meaning, value and purpose. It is precisely the loss of this broader context that creates sadness and grief. This is another reason why IDL interviewing is generally effective at transforming grief and sadness. As you access authentic perspectives that personify contexts that include your own, including your sadness and grief, but transcend them in that they themselves are not feeling sadness or grief, you slowly grow into objectivity regarding your own sadness and grief.

Another approach is to allow yourself to read the words of those who have learned to objectify their feelings, including sadness and grief. An excellent example is the famous Stoic philosopher Marcus Aurelius who has excellent advice that echoes down through the ages: "The first rule is to keep an untroubled spirit. The second is to look things in the face and know them for what they are." "Here is a rule to remember when anything tempts you to feel bitter: not, "This is a misfortune," but "To bear this worthily is good fortune."

Remember to name what you are feeling: "I am feeling sad; I am feeling grief at my loss." Naming objectifies your feeling; it no longer defines you. Instead, it is something that you are experiencing, something that you are perceiving and observing. Consequently, you are not as subjectively immersed in your feeling as you were before you named it. Naming moves you out of the Drama Triangle and into the role of Helper simply through observation of the drama in which you are immersed. You will not be completely free, but you will be able to tell a difference. With repeated naming, you will slowly move yourself into a perspective in which you can view your grief and sadness with loving kindness.

10: Ways Feelings Keep You Stuck in Drama

Confusion

Nobody likes to be confused. It creates a sense of powerlessness that can put us in the role of Victim. Therefore, we avoid confusion or pretend that we aren't confused when we really are. Knowledge, clarity, and wisdom become Rescuers. The quick, confident answer or action becomes our savior even when we are creating a disaster for ourselves.

We sometimes retreat into confusion as a form of self-rescuing from difficult decisions. If you stay confused, you don't have to choose; if you don't choose, you won't risk making a bad choice and thereby avoid feeling even more a Victim. If you view confusion as a Persecutor, are you not turning yourself into a Victim in the search for Rescuers? Is not your negative reaction to your confusion a reflection of your ignorance? Are you recognizing your confusion it for what it is, a wake-up call that is telling you to slow down and get re-oriented?

If you view your confusion as just another wake-up call, then you won't use it to pressure yourself into the Drama Triangle. Listen to your confusion! It will tell you what information you need to become less confused.

10: Ways Feelings Keep You Stuck in Drama

Happiness and Joy

Happiness and joy are not in themselves rescuing feelings. In fact, they are healing, balancing and transformative when they are not a means of avoiding, ignoring or minimizing some challenge. The problem only arises when we use happiness and joy to rescue ourselves from some discomfort, insecurity, failure, or responsibility. Because in such instances the happiness or joy support avoidance, it becomes corrupt; it becomes a Persecutor, trapping you more deeply in the Drama Triangle.

How could such good and valuable emotions as happiness and joy possibly put you in the Drama Triangle? Don't they help you get *out* of it? Because we naturally seek experiences that make us feel happy and joyful, happiness and joy can function as Rescuers. Why? Who wants to feel unhappy, sad, angry, or scared? As with all Rescuers, when happiness and joy are being used as avenues of escape, they only provide the illusion of help. In time they fade, often leading to a painful despondency and a craving addiction for a return to the Lost Paradise of good feelings. Instead of helping us learn to deeply listen to whatever we are avoiding, happiness and joy in such cases conspire with us to avoid ourselves.

When you feel happiness or joy watch to see if any of the three roles of the Drama Triangle are present. Not only do happiness and joy rescue you from a grey, boring, unhappy life; they can act as Persecutors by blinding you to the reality of suffering of others. Seeing that suffering does not mean that you should lose your happiness and joy, but it does mean that you need to differentiate between happiness and joy that rescues and that which does not. In addition, happiness and joy can cause you to throw caution to the wind and make terrible choices in partners or actions.

How do I know if I am using happiness and joy in such a way? Ask yourself,

"What are the main ways that I seek out happiness and joy day-to-day?" Let us say that your answers are "Checking emails, social media, talking with friends, eating chocolate and sex." You then can ask yourself, "What, if anything, am I avoiding when I do these activities?" "Does the resulting happiness and joy I derive from them increase my general happiness and joy or do they just keep me from feeling worse?"

When happiness and joy are used for avoidance or to keep you from feeling worse you are probably living your life on an emotional roller-coaster. There's not much that is healthy about it, although it is very common and very understandable. It is healthy in three year old children, who are their emotions, their preferences and are not using happiness and joy to avoid anything. While you may wish you could live your life as a three year old, how realistic is that? Happiness and joy are like good, strong, healthy horses in charge of a chariot in which you are riding; if you don't keep hold of the reins and provide direction, they will drag you and themselves over a cliff.

11: Words that Keep You Stuck in Drama

Some words put you in the Drama Triangle, whether you speak them or think them. You can't use them and stay out of the Drama Triangle. Because you can't use them and have inner peace, they are to be avoided.

Words that put you in the role of Victim

"Can't"

We often use "can't" to excuse ourselves from someone's request: "I would love to come, but I can't." Are you unable to come or is the truth that you don't want to or you have another appointment? What's keeping you from just saying you have another appointment?

"Couldn't" does the same. It tells others and yourself that you are powerless. "I would have come, but I couldn't." No; you *could* have; no one was holding you prisoner. If you have a conflict, just say you have a conflict. Instead of using "can't," substitute words like, "won't," "choose not to," "will not," or "do not want to." These may take some getting used to; they may feel too strong or powerful. That's because you may not be used to feeling strong or powerful. Use them and you'll grow into it.

"Can't" puts you into the role of Victim because it says, "I am powerless, unable, helpless." Do not use it. If you do, you will not only be telling yourself, "I am a victim;" you will be telling everyone else that you expect them to treat you like you are a Victim. If you use "can't," don't be surprised when people either try to rescue you or take advantage of your powerlessness. They are treating you the way you've told them to treat you.

Ask others to point out to you when you use the word "can't." Your friends and family members can help you create a Drama-free culture at home and at work.

11: Words that Keep You Stuck in Drama

Words that put you in the role of Persecutor

Always

"Always" puts you in the role of Persecutor because it says, "perfection." Perfection does not exist in reality. If the person you are talking to can find only one instance that disproves "always" they have grounds to dismiss what you are saying and stop listening to you. "You are always late," can be disproved by only one instance in which the person was on time. "I am always thoughtful," can be disproved by only one instance in which you were not thoughtful.

If you use "always" you will teach other people to expect you to be an opinionated, unrealistic, unreasonable person who doesn't listen to others. If you use "always," don't be surprised when other people don't want to share what they really think or feel with you, because they don't want you to make them wrong.

Whenever you think "always" you are holding yourself or the world to some unrealistic standard of perfectionism. The result is inevitably self-criticism within the Drama Triangle. Don't use "always." Instead use words like "usually," or "mostly." They communicate that you are confident, but not certain or rigid. They indicate that you believe you can defend your position but that it is not unchangeable.

Never

Like "always," "never" puts you in the role of Persecutor because it says, "perfection." Perfection does not exist in reality, because there are instances that disprove "never." "You are never reliable," can be disproved by only one instance in which you were reliable. "I am never unkind," can be disproved by only one instance in which you were unkind.

When you use "never" you teach people to expect you to be an opinionated, unrealistic, unreasonable person who doesn't listen to others. If you use it, don't be surprised when other people don't want to share what they really think or feel with you, because they don't want you to make them wrong. You are also communicating to them that you are uninterested in holding a rational discussion that is based on facts but instead want to overwhelm their arguments with the power of your irrational emotions.

People use "always" and "never" because they convey the intense feelings that they have. It *feels* like "always" or "never." On a level of emotion and belief, always and never are true! That's the problem. Feelings can indeed be true and still be irrational. What you want is to cultivate feelings that are true and also rational, in that they promote health and well-being. Those feelings that do not are intense reactions; they are inaccurate and they lack credibility. To use words that express intense feelings strengthens those extreme feelings while destroying your credibility and increasing your emotional reactivity. When you change your words to conditional and less extreme expressions, you will also find that you learn to have more control over your feelings. They will no longer rule your life, determine your happiness, make others so defensive, or cause you so much unhappiness.

Don't use "never." Instead use words like "rarely," or "infrequently." Like "usually" and "mostly," they communicate that you are confident, but not certain or rigid. They indicate that you believe you can defend your position but that it is not unchangeable.

Blame

Searching for someone to blame is a favorite defense for those who feel persecuted. They are saying, "I am in the role of Victim, and there's someone or something to blame for it!" Blaming is an avoidance strategy and a logical fallacy because it changes the subject from the truth of the argument to the character or motives of someone else, which is called an *ad hominem* logical fallacy. Rather than solving any problem, blaming only wastes time while making your problem worse. Where there was one problem before, now there are two. The first problem is what you are attempting to avoid dealing with by blaming: "You left your underwear on the floor again!" The blaming creates your second problem: a snipe hunt that changes the subject without doing anything to solve the original problem. A better response would be, "What are you willing to differently so you do not leave your underwear on the floor in the future?"

When you blame others you are making it more likely that they will eventually blame you. If you want to live in a relationship, family, and culture in which you are blamed and in which, instead of solving problems you remain mired in the suffering of the Drama Triangle, by all means, continue to use the world "blame."

You can't blame someone else without blaming yourself. When you blame others you are inevitably blaming those parts of yourself that they represent. This means you can't persecute someone else without persecuting yourself. Do you want to do that? Do you deserve abuse?

Blaming is a problem focus. Simply agreeing to no longer blame shifts communication to a solution focus. After apartheid, South Africa set up a noble alternative to national and personal blaming when, instead of persecuting the malefactors, it set up a Truth and Reconciliation Committee. The idea was for wrong-doers and perpetrators to acknowledge their misdeeds, take responsibility, and take actions that demonstrated a desire to help their society grow into greater health. Isn't finding workable solutions what matters? How does blaming anyone make anything better? Can you force anyone to take responsibility? Do you think you will feel better because you make someone feel worse? Perhaps you will feel better because someone gets punished, but will anything get better? Aren't you just reinforcing a culture of recrimination and blame?

Blaming is an immature habit, similar to children arguing over whose fault it was a glass of milk got knocked over. The best way to break it is to name it, but to do so in a way that doesn't sound like another case of blaming. Instead of saying, "You're blaming again," say, "It sounds to me like you may be blaming. Are you?" This shifts the conversation from your behavior to the subtext of the nature of communication itself. Instead of allowing the emotional cognitive distortion of blaming to become the center of attention by defending against it, you question its legitimacy as a method of communication.

You will break your habit of blaming much more rapidly if you enlist the help of those around you, inviting them to call you out if they hear you blaming. This is because blaming is an act of a Persecutor in the Drama Triangle, and Persecutors notoriously, chronically and sanctimoniously defend the righteousness of their abusive actions. When you blame yourself you will feel completely justified in doing so. It takes help and persistence to break this deeply engrained habit that most of us learned when we were three.

Fault

Get the word "fault" out of your vocabulary today. Why? It can't be used without implying blame. Finding fault is not the same as objectively looking for mistakes, confusions, or deletions. Instead, it involves looking for such things and then *blaming*. Instead of focusing on solutions, fault-finders have to tell others what they've done wrong. Why do we find fault? Like all Persecutors in the Drama Triangle, we generally think we are performing a teaching function. We justify fault-finding as "feedback," "information," or "help." We see themselves as "helpers." Are we? To make that determination, go through the Rescuer checklist: Was your feedback requested? Was the information you gave helpful and appreciated? Did you stop finding fault when the other person told you it wasn't helpful or appreciated? If the answer to any of these questions is "no," then the information you are giving is not "feedback," "information," or "help." It is fault-finding, and you are in the role of Persecutor, but denying it. You don't see yourself as a Persecutor because you don't want to take responsibility for the fact that you are making yourself feel right or powerful at the expense of someone else – most probably someone you love.

If you need to criticize, ask permission. Say something like, "Something you did really irritates/upsets/concerns me, but I don't want to get into the role of Persecutor about it. I want to tell you so it doesn't happen again, but I don't want to make it your fault." Wait and see what they say. They will probably reluctantly give you permission.

If you think this is too much trouble and instead continue to point out the weaknesses and failures of others in a way they view as fault-finding, don't be surprised when others lie to you about what they have done or not done in order to avoid your criticism. Don't be surprised when others look for opportunities to find fault with you, as a way to take revenge for what they view as unfair attacks. Don't be surprised when others distance themselves from you to protect themselves. Don't be surprised when others are not there when you need them. Don't be surprised when you find the same patterns of alienation of affection repeating with new relationships, because it's not the other person who is the problem; it's because you're stuck in the Drama Triangle and you would rather find fault in others and yourself than get out.

Should

"Should" implies conscience, parents, God, church, script, obligation, permission from authorities, and guilt. If you enjoy feeling guilty, if you want to make someone else feel guilty in order to manipulate them to get them to do what you want, use "should" and "shouldn't."

This pernicious verb is often used to express externally imposed rules and laws. You "shouldn't" jay-walk; you "should" brush your teeth. You "shouldn't" fart in public; you "should" obey your parents. When you tell yourself you "should" do something, you put the full weight of some moral code on your shoulders, like Moses carrying the Ten Commandments down from Mount Sinai. Everyone benefits from having a moral code. How about allowing people to have one that they choose? Isn't that what you demand for yourself? When you act out of your moral code, how about doing so because it's helpful, not because you "should?" Start asking yourself, "Am I doing this because it's something that's helpful to myself or others or because I "should?"

"Should" also has the function of rescuing you from guilt and shame since, if you do what you are expected to do, you are blameless. This mechanism has been used since time immemorial by parents to get children to behave. Once children have internalized the tyranny of "should" they will parent themselves, making the jobs of moms and dads, teachers and police much easier. Society uses "should" to great benefit to get citizens to obey laws so that society runs more smoothly and authority is not questioned, giving autocrats of all kinds a free ride.

How about all those things that you *have* to do that you don't want to do, like paying taxes, showing up in court, flossing, going to work, and obeying your boss? First, recognize that you don't *have* to do any of those things; it's just that the alternatives are worse. If you look at them objectively, you do these things because they are in your own best interest. You are doing them for yourself. Once you get clear on this, you can own the fact that you want to do them more than you don't want to do them, not because you *should*.

"Should" and "shouldn't" create inner resistance that makes it more difficult to do things you don't want to do or have to do. Once you recognize that you have a choice and that you are doing whatever you do because it is helping yourself or someone else, your resistance will become a lot less. It may even vanish entirely. You will then spend your life doing things that make your life and the lives of others, more productive, relatively outside the Drama Triangle, rather than doing things you should do, and spending your life feeling oppressed, in the Victim role of the Drama Triangle.

When you use "should" and "shouldn't" you put yourself in all three roles of the Drama Triangle. You not only get to feel you are a helpless Victim, but you get to find Persecutors everywhere: work, municipal hall, police, other drivers, your parents, your partner. They are all "shoulding" on you. Even your kids become Persecutors, because after all, you "should" help them with their homework and make sure they grow up to be good people.

You cannot use "should" and be out of the Drama Triangle. Instead, it instantaneously places you in the role of Persecutor. Hopefully, that alone is enough of a reason for you to swear off its use. By all means, ask family and those at work to call you on it when they hear you using "should." By doing so, you will help those in your immediate environment to stop using it as well, which is a big step toward creating a daily life and work culture that is not contaminated with the Drama Triangle.

Ought

Everything above regarding "should" applies to "ought." However, "ought" might be a bit more compelling and have a bit more of the Persecutor about it. Who gave you the right to play the role of conscience? Stop using "ought." It's toxic.

Must

"Must" implies, "Don't think; don't question; don't doubt; just DO what you *have* to do." "Must" creates a double bind. For example, if you are in the military, you "must" obey your superiors. If you don't, very bad things happen to you. However, if your military superiors order you to do something illegal, like torture, and you get caught, you will go to jail, not your superiors. If you "must" do your homework to pass a class, then you risk spending your life beating yourself with a stick, so to speak, to make yourself work. What do you get for that? In order to succeed you will keep yourself under constant stress. Even if you make good grades as a result, you will have no peace of mind.

11: Words that Keep You Stuck in Drama

When you use "must," you put yourself in the same type of moral vice that "ought," "should," "fault" and "blame" generate. You create for yourself a guaranteed "lose-lose" situation, where you are going to end up feeling bad, regardless of what you do. When you use "must" with others, you are almost guaranteed to be viewed as a Persecutor. You are also almost guaranteeing that the other person will resent you and will do whatever you want with passive or active resistance, meaning that it will not be done well. Parents typically find themselves in this situation with their children and wonder why.

What do you do when something *must* be done? How can you avoid these problems? With children, give them a choice they can't refuse: "Would you prefer to do your homework or vacuum the house?" "Do you want to get up on time to catch the bus to school or would you prefer to walk?" "Would you prefer to clean your room or clean the toilets?" With those adults that you supervise, just make whatever needs to be done a matter of policy, part of their job description. You are not requiring that they do it; it's part of their employment description. They don't have to do it; only if they want to keep their job. With a partner, talk about the consequences if they don't do it: "You don't have to pick up after yourself if you don't want to, and I don't have to cook you dinner if I don't want to." Not too subtle. They will probably get the message. If they accuse you of blackmail, say, "What do you think would be appropriate consequences if you don't pick up after yourself?"

But

When "but" is used in sentences it negates what has been said before the "but." If you say, "I can be very thoughtful, but I can forget really important things," what are you really saying? You are emphasizing that you can forget really important things. You are also teaching the other person that if they need to criticize you, they can simply remind you that you forget really important things. If you say, "I love you, but I can't stand it when you are late," what are you really saying? You are saying that your intolerance is more important than your love. You are also teaching the other person that if they want to get you mad, all they have to do is be late.

When you use "but" you are contradicting what you just said before the "but." Not only is that crazy-making and confusing; it is a form of self-persecution or persecution of the other person within the Drama Triangle. Sometimes we reverse the abuse to lessen its impact: "You are a real jackass, but I love you anyway." This is a complement with a hook in it. You are still in the role of Persecutor, making the other person into a Victim.

These examples show that using "but" either mixes pepper into the honey of your words or is designed to make you appear truthful, honest, or loving by sugarcoating the medicine you are dishing out. In either case, it rarely works. It just sends a mixed message. What to do?

Why not simply eliminate "but" and use "and" instead? Why not simply say, "I can be very thoughtful, *and* I can forget really important things." Why not just say, "I love you, *and* I can't stand it when you are late." Why not say, "You are a real jackass, *and* I love you anyway."

If you will make this simple change you will find that you are clearer and speak with more confidence. It will also be a small step toward moving you out of the Drama Triangle.

Words that may put you in the role of Rescuer

"Need" and "Want"

"Need" sounds like a perfectly helpful and honest word. You "need" to get things done; you "need" to do your homework; you "need" to set goals; you "need" to be respectful, you "need" to help others. When you "need" to do something, who are you doing it for, others or for yourself? You are doing it for yourself, not the other person because you are the one with the need. However, this is not the normal implication of the word "need." It generally implies outside compulsion, something someone or something has imposed upon us. The feeling it conveys is similar to "must," with all the problems mentioned above that it entails.

When you say, "You need to clean your room," you are posing as mind-reader. Do you know that your child *needs* to clean his or her room? Don't you mean that you *want* them to clean their room? If that is the case, why don't you say so? Probably because you want to sound "nice." Instead, you are being unclear, dishonest in your motives, and using language that gets you stuck in the Rescuer role of the Drama Triangle.

This holds true even when you say, "They need me to do this," or, "You need me to help you." What you probably mean to say is that they *want* you to do this or I *want* to help you to do that."

Using "need" can also be an invitation for the other person to climb into the role of Rescuer: "I need you so much!" "I need your help!" Do you need rescuing or do you want help? If you need rescuing, you're saying you need to stay stuck in the Drama Triangle. If you say you want help, then you may actually get help instead of rescuing. Instead of using "need," try using want. It may feel uncomfortable, because it is more direct. It is also more powerful. It expresses more confidence and honest desire.

However, both "need" and "want" can be used to justify indulging in a craving and thereby jumping into the role of Victim, with food, others, drink, or cigarettes in the role of Rescuer. In such a case, a cognitive distortion is at work. That is because you don't "need" a substance or activity that kills you; you don't really *want* a substance or activity that kills you; it just *feels* like you do. By using "need" or "want" in this way you are strengthening your emotional and physical cravings. Instead, use words that reflect preference but with less intensity: "I would like some chocolate"; "I would prefer it if you would repeat what I said so I know I was clear in what I said to you."

Because using "want" and "need" in these very common ways is a cognitive distortion, you need a substitute thought or statement, such as, "I don't need/want this cigarette; my *body/needy emotions* need/want this cigarette." The basic question to ask is, "Do I want/need this so much that it's worth it to me to jump into Victim role in the Drama Triangle?" "Do I want/need to be a Victim?"

"Need" and "want" put you into all three roles of the Drama Triangle. Because they imply compulsion, you risk being in the role of Persecutor. If you feel persecuted by a demand associated with some need, you may be placing yourself in the role of Victim. If you are helping others because you "need" to, you are probably in the role of Rescuer.

12: Conscience and the Drama Triangle

Conscience is your still small voice, the one that tells you right from wrong and good from bad. It is your connection to God. Your conscience keeps you from sin. Without conscience you are an animal, without guidance, ethics, morals, or social norms. If you would only listen to it and follow it, you would be happy. Humanity's perversity is its failure to listen to and do the bidding of its conscience.

Or so they say. Conscience is perhaps the oldest, most hallowed bit of delusion in the consciousness of humanity. To question it is to go against God, society, the soul, the Good, religion, and love. What could be worse? What could be more blasphemous?

Whenever you try to make yourself do something you don't want to do or not do something that you want to do, are you listening to your conscience? Conscience is mother's milk laced with small, regular doses of heroin. The crack is not enough to kill you, but enough to addict you when you are still too young to remember it happening. The rewards of conformity to conscience as well as the punishments if you disobey it, are strong enough to keep you addicted for your entire life. Marx would have been been more accurate if he had said, "Conscience is the opium of the people."

Isn't the purpose of your conscience to keep you safe and healthy so that you will be a good child, citizen, and child of God? These are the types of good intentions that parents and leaders have. They themselves may not be aware that conscience also has the benefit of being a powerful tool for your socialization and pacification. If I, as your parent, teacher, President or guru can get you to do what I want automatically, because you think it is "God's will" or "conscience," then my life gets a lot easier. You are more likely to obey me and less likely to ask questions, refuse orders, or disobey laws. Whenever your parents, or some religious or spiritual leader want to get you to do something, to think a certain way, or wish to protect themselves behind a shield of unimpeachable credibility, what can they do? Can't they present themselves as the voice of conscience?

Can't conscience be a good thing? How about "Eat your vegetables," or, "Don't play in the street." Such statements are not conscience but rather simple pieces of information, called "injunctions," given for rational reasons, like health and safety. However, if they are given with threat of punishment ("....or else!") or with a serving of "should," "ought," "must," and guilt, they are conscience and abusive, because they are Persecutors that create and maintain the Drama Triangle in your thoughts and relationships.

Most people will tell you that what is *really* conscience is the same for everyone. However, isn't it true that conscience differs according to culture, religions, social norms and mores? Won't most Christians and Jews argue that their conscience is different from the Islamic conscience? Isn't that what the branding of Islam as terroristic claims? Won't Arabs and other people in countries bombed by the US and NATO argue that people in the West either have no conscience or a very different sense of what conscience means, if conscience allows them to do such things?

When you listen to and follow your conscience are you thinking for yourself? Are you instead following the internalized moral precepts of your family, culture and religion? Have you not so completely internalized them that you *think* their injunctions are your conscience? The inculcation of the vast majority of what is called "conscience" is a loving process of abuse and victimization within the Drama Triangle. Parents and cultures everywhere find the internalization of social values, called "socialization," as conscience highly useful. Someday it will be widely recognized as such and parents will teach their children not only the difference between conscience and their life compass, but how to find, listen to, and follow their life compass. They will learn how to beware of anyone or anything that claims to speak as their conscience.

"Life compass" is a term used by Integral Deep Listening (IDL) to refer to consensus perspectives and recommendations you access by interviewing the personifications of dream characters and life issues that are important to you. These perspectives, called "emerging potentials," are not the children of your parents, culture, religion or society like you are. They have their own priorities and are not afraid to disagree with yours and the voice of your conscience. You can listen to both your conscience and interviewed emerging potentials, compare them and decide for yourself which has your greatest good as its primary interest.

You are the product of a number of beliefs that you had to accept to survive, adapt, and grow in your family and school. Weren't you much less likely to disobey if the preferences of your parents, teachers and society were called

12: Conscience and the Drama Triangle

"conscience" and you were told that this was something innate within you, or the same as God's will? To trespass against your conscience may be a threat to your society, religion, or family, and therefore a threat to you, when you are punished for disobeying authority figures.

Conscience presents itself as acting in your own good. It knows what is best for you and tells you its actions are only because it cares about and loves you. It is selfless, and you ignore it at your own peril. How is this different from a Rescuer in the Drama Triangle who tells you, "I know what you need. I am only trying to help you. If you don't listen to me you are ungrateful and foolish."

Conscience carries the marks not of a Helper, but of a Rescuer within the Drama Triangle. Rescuers are not Helpers, because they mask self-interest behind a facade of care for others. They do not ask if their help is needed, they do not check to see if the help they are giving is useful, and they do not stop "helping," preferring self-martyrdom and burn-out to recognition of their selfishness.

Your conscience knows what is good for you and speaks up without you asking. It doesn't check to see if its voice is helping, because it knows that it, by its nature, is helping. It doesn't have to check. It refuses to stop demanding you follow it, unless you shut it out with a drug or some other type of intense avoidant stimulation.

Conscience as Rescuer promotes its truth, way, thoughts, feelings, perspectives, and actions, not yours, and certainly not the priorities of your life compass. Your life compass, revealed by interviewing your emerging potentials as they manifest as dream characters and the personifications of your life issues, balances and evolves confidence, empathy, wisdom, acceptance, and witnessing within yourself. Unlike conscience, it is selfless. If the priorities of your life compass and conscience happen to coincide it is coincidence, not due to any awareness or intention of your conscience.

On yet closer examination, you will find that your conscience not only is not your friend, it is never was or has been your friend. This is because it never wants you to listen to yourself. It only wants you to listen to *it*. Your conscience doesn't trust you. It doesn't respect your judgment. It doesn't even like you unless you are doing what *it* wants. How is this different from the role of Persecutor in the Drama Triangle which tells you, "I am only punishing you for your own good"? Isn't it amazing that you continue to give your conscience any attention or any respect at all?

Persecutors do not see themselves as persecutors. They only say what they say for your own good; they only do what they do because they love you. This means that if your parents or teachers yell at you or call you ugly, stupid, or a failure, it is only for your own good. Verbal abuse in the name of conscience is not verbal abuse at all; it is "character strengthening," and if you knew what was good for you, you would agree with it and change.

12: Conscience and the Drama Triangle

If you examine your conscience closely, you will discover that it is the Persecutor role in the Drama Triangle masquerading as the Rescuer, which is itself masquerading as a Helper. Your conscience is deception wrapped in deception; is there any surprise that so many believe in it and that so few ever free themselves from it? How many people ever stop to ask themselves, "How much of what I call my conscience is different from what my parents, culture or this or that peer group believes?" How much of what I call my conscience is probably internalized social and cultural norms?"

When rulers, people, and nations declare war on you in the name of God and then bomb you, destroy your towns, scatter cancer-causing munitions-grade uranium all over your fields, rape your wife and daughters, and torture you to death, is it not for the greater good, for democracy, justice and God, because conscience dictates? People who believe in conscience and then do such things have a very high rate of suicide. As of this writing, the suicide rate of American military veterans is currently twenty-two a day, about one every hour. There is one suicide a day among active duty US military, all among people acting on the basis of "conscience." This is because their conscience has contradicted their life compass on such a fundamental level that there is no way to rationalize away the discrepancy. Unable to escape the cognitive dissonance, but unable, unwilling, or ignorant of how to free themselves of the tyranny of conscience, they kill themselves in an attempt at self-rescue.

How to escape conscience? There is no alternative to sorting through your thoughts, feelings, and motives, one by one, and finding out which script injunctions you carry that are informational facts and which are guilt-creating, persecutorial, "shoulds," "oughts," and "musts." This is why IDL has chapters in *Waking Up* both on recognizing and freeing yourself from your life script as well as on the major emotional cognitive distortions. If you want to learn to think for yourself you must exorcise the internalized toxic directives of the ghosts of your parents that are living rent-free in your attic. Keep the nurturing voices of your parents but evict the rest!

Your conscience is never, ever representative of your life compass. How do you tell the difference? If you will learn to interview your emerging potentials you will slowly learn to differentiate between your life compass and conscience. Your life compass doesn't do drama. It's not in the Drama Triangle. It works to balance confidence, empathy, wisdom, acceptance, inner peace, and witnessing. If you don't follow it, it doesn't threaten you or try to make you feel guilty any more than a compass that points north cares if you go east or south. However, when you do follow your life compass, life gets easier. You have a deep inner sense that you are on the right path for your life. You will have a confidence in who you are and where you are headed regardless of what others may think or say. You will be able to speak and act with authority because you will be in alignment with what is

12: Conscience and the Drama Triangle

true, good and harmonious for you. As you move into this sacred space you outgrow any need for conscience, not because you no longer listen to it, but because you subject its voice to a higher, more authentic authority that is uniquely your own.

A debate between believers and non-believers in conscience

"Conscience is the light by which we interpret the will of God in our own lives."
Thomas Merton

"The torture of a bad conscience is the hell of a living soul."
John Calvin

"[T]he infliction of cruelty with a good conscience is a delight to moralists. That is why they invented Hell."
Bertrand Russell

(Russell is universally hated by all those who cannot or will not think.)

"There comes a time when one must take a position that is neither safe, nor politic, nor popular, but he must take it because conscience tells him it is right."
Martin Luther King, Jr.

(Conscience is a very poor, unreliable reason to do what is right, if only because your worst enemy appeals to the same justification. Doing what is right? For who? Under what circumstances?)

"If all the world hated you and believed you wicked, while your own conscience approved of you and absolved you from guilt, you would not be without friends."

12: Conscience and the Drama Triangle

Charlotte Brontë

(If you do what you think is right you don't have to care whether it makes sense or is useful.)

"Conscience is what makes a boy tell his mother before his sister does."
Evan Esar

"Guilt is also a way for us to express to others that we are a person of good conscience.
Tom Hodgkinson

(The conscience of the personality disordered and of the two year old are both free of guilt.)

"Your conscience is the measure of the honesty of your selfishness. Listen to it carefully."
Richard Bach

(This is very true, but probably not in the sense Bach means it. Because conscience wants what is best for itself, and not for your life compass, it is not only selfish, but completely honest about its selfishness.)

"Character is doing what you don't want to do but know you should do."
Joyce Meyer

("Should," is a dead giveaway that we are dealing with conscience in the form of the Persecutor role in the Drama Triangle.)

"Betrayal is common for men with no conscience."
Toba Beta

(That is because betrayal is a motive often projected upon others, conscience or no conscience.)

"Let us give ourselves indiscriminately to everything our passions suggest, and we will always be happy…Conscience is not the voice of Nature but only the voice of prejudice."
Marquis de Sade

(The Marquis is feared by purveyors of guilt and conscience everywhere.)

12: Conscience and the Drama Triangle

"The only tyrant I accept in this world is the 'still small voice' within me. And even though I have to face the prospect of being a minority of one, I humbly believe I have the courage to be in such a hopeless minority."

Mahatma Gandhi

(Gandhi, who beat his wife regularly, did so with a clear conscience. Tyrants do not want what is good for you; they do not want what is good for the majority; they only want what is good for them, but mask their selfishness with conscience. Tyrants of all sorts are by nature selfish persecutors, lost in the Drama Triangle.)

"In matters of conscience, the law of the majority has no place."

Mahatma Gandhi

("Forget democracy and consensus governance; I don't care what you think.")

"There is no witness so dreadful, no accuser so terrible as the conscience that dwells in the heart of every man."

Polybius

(For Polybius, conscience is a persecutor and tyrant, but that's a good thing.)

"Conscience is thus explained only as the voice of God in the soul."

Peter Kreeft

(When societal injunctions have the force of God's will and are defined as both your central truth and intuition, then you are transformed into a zombie, the waking dead servant of current cultural preferences.)

"Conscience and cowardice are really the same things, Basil. Conscience is the trade-name of the firm. That is all."

Oscar Wilde

(You don't have to think for yourself or work out difficult moral dilemmas if you appeal to your conscience.)

"Since then your sere Majesty and your Lordships seek a simple answer, I will give it in this manner, neither horned nor toothed. Unless I am convinced by the testimony of the Scriptures or by clear reason (for I do not trust either in the pope or in councils alone, since it is well known that they have often erred and contradicted themselves), I am bound by the Scriptures I have quoted and my conscience is captive to the Word of God. I cannot and I will not recant anything, since it is neither safe nor right to go against conscience. May God help me. Amen."

12: Conscience and the Drama Triangle

(*Reply to the Diet of Worms*, April 18, 1521)"

Martin Luther

(Martin Luther demonstrates that when you follow your conscience, you put yourself on a diet of worms. His conscience produced some of the most discriminatory bile ever to be uttered by a man of God and conscience. See http://ergofabulous.org/luther/)

"Between the radiant white of a clear conscience and the coal black of a conscience sullied by sin lie many shades of gray–where most of us live our lives. Not perfect but not beyond redemption."

Sherry L. Hoppe

(There can never be either integration or union within the framework of the metaphysical dualism that conscience creates and maintains.)

"True law, the code of justice, the essence of our sensations of right and wrong, is the conscience of society. It has taken thousands of years to develop, and it is the greatest, the most distinguishing quality which has developed with mankind ... If we can touch God at all, where do we touch him save in the conscience? And what is the conscience of any man save his little fragment of the conscience of all men in all time?"

Walter Van Tilburg Clark

(A clear expression of conscience as simply the transmission of socio-cultural norms.)

"Conscience is the inner voice that warns us somebody may be looking."

H.L. Mencken

(If you can teach me to fear the consequences of my behavior, based on what you have taught me to call my conscience, I will monitor myself, freeing you and society to do as you will.)

"I have a different idea of elegance. I don't dress like a fop, it's true, but my moral grooming is impeccable. I never appear in public with a soiled conscience, a tarnished honor, threadbare scruples, or an insult that I haven't washed away. I'm always immaculately clean, adorned with independence and frankness. I may not cut a stylish figure, but I hold my soul erect. I wear my deeds as ribbons, my wit is sharper then the finest mustache, and when I walk among men I make truths ring like spurs."

Edmond Rostand

12: Conscience and the Drama Triangle

(Conscience as social propriety.)

"Perhaps conscience did not always produce cowards. Sometimes it made a man feel better about himself."

Robert Ludlum

(Is the purpose of conscience not only to make you feel better about yourself, but to feel superior to all those others you judge as acting less out of conscience?)

"An educator should consider that he has failed in his job if he has not succeeded in instilling some trace of a divine dissatisfaction with our miserable social environment."

Anthony Standen

(Guilt and conscience are the foundations of a good education.)

"It is neither right nor safe to go against my conscience."

Martin Luther

(Since your conscience is a punishing Persecutor, it is unwise to go against it.)

"No guilt is forgotten so long as the conscience still knows of it."

Stefan Zweig

(Conscience as enforcer of guilt.)

"Conscience is no more than the dead speaking to us."

Jim Carroll

(Jim does not mean what he is saying. He means that conscience is the knowledge of the ancients. What he is saying is that conscience is a haunting by voices that seek you to follow their truth, not that of your life compass.)

"The immature conscience is not its own master. It simply parrots the decisions of others. It does not make judgments of its own; it merely conforms to the judgments of others. That is not real freedom, and it makes true love impossible, for if we are to love truly and freely, we must be able to give something that is truly our own to another. If our heart does not belong to us, asks Merton, how can we give it to another?"

Jon Katz

(Jon has drunk the Kool Aid. He still thinks there is such a thing as a good

12: Conscience and the Drama Triangle

conscience.)

"Anybody can be charming if they don't mind faking it, saying all the stupid, obvious, nauseating things that a conscience keeps most people from saying. Happily, I don't have a conscience. I say them."

Jeff Lindsay

(The opposite of conscience is not immorality, as this quote implies; it is the freedom to find and follow your life compass.)

"The study of law can be disappointing at times, a matter of applying narrow rules and arcane procedure to an uncooperative reality; a sort of glorified accounting that serves to regulate the affairs of those who have power–and that all too often seeks to explain, to those who do not, the ultimate wisdom and justness of their condition.

But that's not all the law is. The law is also memory; the law also records a long-running conversation, a nation arguing with its conscience."

Barack Obama

(…a professor of Constitutional law who justifies both the personally ordered murder of civilians with drones, some of whom have been US citizens, in clear violation of both US and international law – all in the name of conscience.)

"The older you get, the more you understand how your conscience works. The biggest and only critic lives in your perception of people's perception of you rather than people's perception of you."

Criss Jami

(Other people are not the cause of your unhappiness; what you tell yourself you should and should not do in the name of conscience is.)

13: How Our World Views Keep Us Stuck in the Drama Triangle

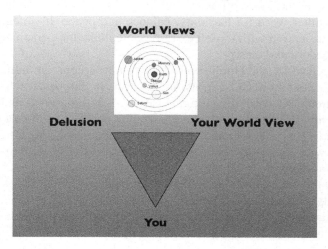

Do you know what your world view is? Do you know what beliefs and realities it is designed to rescue you from? World views are perceptual cognitive distortions, the delusions that generate the context of your life. Consequently, they are difficult to spot because you are subjectively enmeshed in them. Your world view is difficult to change because your entire sense of who you are and why you are alive is determined by it. When you recognize it and question its assumptions you call into question the very foundation of your life. Many people are afraid to do so because they are afraid that the alternative is meaninglessness and nihilism. However, IDL interviewing clearly demonstrates that the exact opposite is the case. The more you free yourself from your world views the more you let go of fundamental perceptual cognitive distortions that keep you stuck in the Drama Triangle.

The world view of the West grows out of Mosaic law (the Ten Commandments in particular), Greek rationalistic dualism and scientific (empirical) humanism. It emphasizes good over evil, right over wrong, godliness over sinfulness, and the scientific over the traditional and metaphysical. It tends to identify with the Rescuer position in the Drama Triangle and the "Good" in the Socratic Triune of the True, the Beautiful and the Good. Its integration in IDL is through identification with those emerging potentials that personify compassion and acceptance, aliveness, service and detachment.

The world view of the shamanistic-Chinese traditions emphasizes societal stability and the balancing of natural forces, harmony over chaos, balance over imbalance, yang over yin and loyalty over selfishness. It tends to identify with the Victim position in the Drama Triangle and the "Beautiful" in the Socratic triune. "Beauty" is another word for harmony, balance and peace. Its integration in IDL is through identification with those emerging potentials that personify inner peace, witnessing, freedom and clarity.

The world view of the Hindu and Buddhist traditions of India emphasizes enlightenment, liberation and life as an illusion. It emphasizes liberation over karma, enlightenment over dreaming, wisdom over ignorance and purity over impurity. It tends to identify with the Persecutor position in the Drama Triangle and "Wisdom" in the Socratic Triune. Its integration in IDL is through identification with those emerging potentials that personify wisdom, confidence, balance and wakefulness.

Shifting from macrocosm to microcosm, all of us grow up within a psychologically geocentric worldview; perceptually, we are the center of our universe. Outgrowing this important assumption of our formative years is a lifelong task that very few complete. You may have an optimistic world view, such as positivity or pessimistic world view of skepticism or nihilism. You may value work over play or comfort over risk. You may value getting along with people over being assertive. In any case, such life positions were generally crafted when you were a child in order to survive in the socio-cultural expectations of your family. Others were developed later, generally in reaction to disillusionments of one sort or another. Today you are most likely living in a different reality than that of your childhood while you remain clinging to an old, outmoded world view of your childhood in important respects. A world view that was designed to rescue you when you were a child may be persecuting you today.

One of the quickest, most effective ways to outgrow a confining world view is to interview perspectives that have different world views than your own. The more you do so the more likely you will be to expand into broader, inclusive perspectives that are relatively out of the Drama Triangle.

18: How Our World Views Keep Us Stuck in the Drama Triangle

Culture

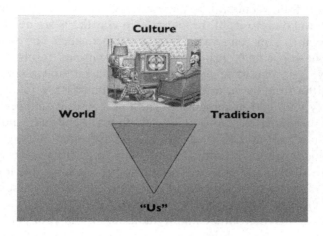

Cultural traditions are wonderful things. The idea of karma has provided social stability within Indian culture for thousands of years. The Jewish belief in being God's Chosen People has helped keep Jews together as a group long after other groups have come and gone. In the United States, the ideas of individual initiative, human rights and capitalism combined to create a model imitated by much of the world. Still, there are intrinsic trade-offs built into any notion of culture. The idea of American "Exceptionalism" has allowed it to exploit and kill Native Americans, Africans, Central and South Americans, Iraqis and just about everybody else, making American culture, in many ways, a Persecutor as well as Rescuer.

You hold certain beliefs that you think are true that you use to make sense of your world and your relationship to it. These beliefs create the cultural context in which you live. Americans tend to believe in individual freedom above government and *laissez faire* capitalism above regulation. In 2017, religious beliefs continue to strongly influence mainstream American culture. Chinese tend to create centralized systems of governmental control of both business and personal life. Europeans tend to place governmental regulation above individual freedoms and to base decisions less on religious motivations than Americans do.

Your culture generally takes the place of your life compass. Instead of finding and listening to your own emerging potentials, you follow the assumptions of your culture. They are supposed to guide you and protect you—in short, to play the role of Rescuer. The problem is that your cultural assumptions often differ from your life compass because they serve different ends. Culture generally

18: How Our World Views Keep Us Stuck in the Drama Triangle

reinforces social solidarity while the priorities of your life compass may or may not. When you follow cultural assumptions that do not reflect the ways life is attempting to wake up to itself through you, a conflict is set up that turns culture into a Persecutor. Your cultural assumptions then keep you from finding and following your life's path, instead substituting various forms of self-rescuing. Consequently, it is important to know what your cultural assumptions are and where they differ from the priorities of your life compass.

You identify with both macrocosmic and microcosmic cultures. On a personal level, your culture involves your beliefs about work and play and how you treat others. It includes not merely what you believe and intend but also what you say you believe and what you actually do and don't do. Many people say they believe in one set of values while practicing another. We often do this toward ourselves when we are kind to others and critical of ourselves, treating ourselves in ways we wouldn't treat others or allow others to treat us.

The analogy to macrocosmic cultural traditions within your personal culture are your habits. They create stability and comfort, rescuing you from instability and discomfort while insulating you from the disruption of other influences that are a threat to your own culture. In time, that insulating cocoon of comfortable expectations and ritualistic routine suffocates you. At that point, the culture that rescued you by giving you an identity and a place in society has become your persecutor.

Most people are victims of their cultures, yet tenaciously cling to exactly what is suppressing their freedom. Jared Diamond, in *Collapse,* describes this self-destructive reality throughout history, using the Mayan civilization in Central America, Easter Islanders and Viking settlers in Greenland as examples of self-generated cultural collapse.

IDL unearths your largely hidden underlying cultural assumptions by comparing and contrasting them with the cultures assumed by the perspectives of interviewed emerging potentials. The process of simply listening to and becoming alternative perspectives clarifies and transforms cultural assumptions that otherwise condition our happiness and growth outside our awareness.

What is your personal culture? How do you use it to help you stay secure and stable so you can live your life? How does your personal culture wall you off from challenging influences that you need to grow to the next level in your life?

18: How Our World Views Keep Us Stuck in the Drama Triangle

Religion

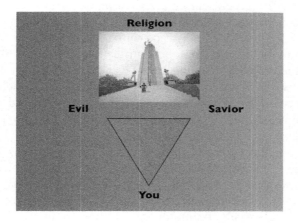

Do you use religion to give your life meaning and purpose? Religion, as societal culture rather than personal spirituality, is intended to rescue us from meaninglessness, selfishness and even evil by promising some sort of salvation: *nirvana, samadhi,* the end of karma, heaven with Mohammed or the Messiah, or hanging out with the angels and Jesus in Heaven after the Last Judgment. Religion teaches us to do all sorts of socially-sanctioned activities to reach salvation: say our prayers, meditate, do good, help others, go to church, temple, mosque or synagogue, obey our elders, follow God's laws, tithe and respect the leaders of our religion.

All of this is good and important at prepersonal and early personal levels of development, when our sense of self is either not yet consolidated or based on group norms. However, as we develop into mid-personal reason and beyond collective religious forms normally decrease in importance as we first place more emphasis on our own individual search for freedom, unity and inner peace and secondly, thin our identification with our prior definitions of self.

In today's world, there are a myriad of options other than religion that meet these needs that either did not exist in the past or were prohibited by heavy social sanctions. The more people wake up to these new alternatives the more church, temple, synagogue and mosque attendance shrinks and the more alternative world views take the place traditionally allotted in society to religion. We could therefore say that our world view is our religion, but it is probably more accurate to say that religions are examples of world views, of which there are a number that are not particularly religious.

This trend toward the embracing of non-religious world views is accelerating,

18: How Our World Views Keep Us Stuck in the Drama Triangle

and there is not much religion can do about it, although they constantly try by redefining ancient truths in contemporary contexts. Believers invariably contend that their understanding, representing their current level of development, is what the scriptures and founders "really" meant.

While church leaders, messiahs and gurus may appear as some of your interviewed dream characters and personifications of your life issues, most interviewed characters will be found to have little to do with religion. This can come as quite a shock to the religiously and metaphysically inclined, because it undercuts their assumptions about what is and is not spiritual and what spirituality entails. For example, an interviewed toilet brush may be found to possess as much or more sacred meaning as an interviewed angel or guru.

As with culture in general, your life compass is not the same as socially-created religion. While it is indeed possible to relate to religion from outside the Drama Triangle and to find core religious values that are shared with interviewed emerging potentials, religion itself tends to function within the Drama Triangle. This is because religious communities are bigger than we are, and our participation places us within its collective world view, which as a perceptual cognitive distortion provides a context within the Drama Triangle. Therefore, participating in any religion while staying out of the Drama Triangle is not easy. Most people who believe they can become adherents of a faith without falling into the Drama Triangle end up deluding themselves. Recognize and respect your own limitations.

Religion functions in the role of Persecutor at least as much as it is in the role of Rescuer. Although religion does its best to hide it and not talk about it, Persecution occurs chiefly in the form of the exceptionalism and exclusivity which is endemic to all forms of religion. Each religion says, "We love and accept you unconditionally – as long as you agree with us. If you do not, you are at best, a second class citizen and at worst, a threat, to be scapegoated, cast out, and punished." From religious wars to severe penalties to those who break religious law, from discriminating against unbelievers to expelling those who do not conform, religion has traditionally played a major role in dispensing abuse in the name of spirituality. This does not make religion bad or wrong, but rather something to be used with respect for its ability to ensnare us in drama.

*18: How Our World Views Keep Us Stuck
in the Drama Triangle*

Hinduism

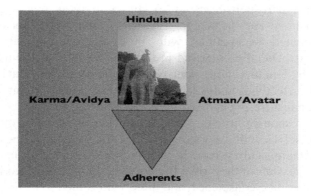

In polytheistic Hinduism you theoretically have a wide variety of Rescuers to choose from, including Brahma, Vishnu, Siva, Krishna and Hanuman, just to name a few. Practically, you will worship the gods favored by your Vaishnavite, Shaivite, Shaktivite or Brahmanistic sect, which is determined by the caste and family into which you were born. Hinduism also offers a wide variety of spiritual disciplines, yogas and purification rituals to rescue you from bad karma while allowing you to accrue good karma so that you will be reborn next life into a higher caste or circumstances generally more favorable for *moksha*, or freedom from the ultimate persecution, *samsara,* or the wheel of rebirth.

Persecution is not only provided by your own bad karma but more fundamentally by your own ignorance. Therefore, it is important that you seek wisdom by studying the scriptures and becoming a *chela,* or spiritual disciple, of a spiritual path or a teacher, guru, living or dead, who has attained *samadhi* and knows the way to *moksha.* While gods, rituals and disciplines provide preliminary rescuing, the real rescuing is provided by your guru, who will show you how to attain to the awareness that your True Self, or *Atman,* is God, or *Brahman*.

Beneath this sophisticated metaphysic, which continues to attract adherents in the West, are the impressive social benefits of Hinduism. It has largely been responsible for the relative stability of India for over three thousand years, largely by convincing people that they chose their birth conditions, family and life experiences based on their deeds in past lives. Therefore, they are exactly where they have put themselves and are in the life circumstances that they have "earned." It is through conforming with those birth conditions and learning the lessons that their culture and society have to teach them that they gain the good karma that allows a rebirth into more favorable circumstances.

Adherents of Hinduism take personal responsibility for their life circumstances even when external social injustices are the root cause of their suffering. Belief in predestined personal responsibility is so strong in India that even though the highly discriminatory and persecutory caste system, which locks people into socially pre-ordained occupations with little chance of financial or social advancement, was officially outlawed in India in 1950, it still remains largely in place, enforced by Hindu culture, society and religion. In this regard, the karma-caste system has effectively reduced the blaming of society, religious or political leaders for personal suffering and any absence of human rights.

By taking all responsibility for their circumstances upon themselves, Hindus have made themselves willing Victims within the Drama Triangle of a highly persecutorial metaphysical system. Is the *dharma,* or universal law that governs their lives an expression of their own life compass or is it imposed by society and culture, internalized like conscience, and merely presumed to be their own truth?

In such a system, government, society and priests do not have a primary responsibility to the people, but to working out their own karma by fulfilling the duties associated with their caste and their societal roles. This is an example of how believing, "If it is to be, it is up to me," is a grandiose statement of personal control within a world and life that is conditioned by circumstances of birth, culture, society, geography and disease. Hinduism and similar systems such as Buddhism, Jainism and Sikhism therefore make us Victims of our own unrealistic sense of personal responsibility. The result is that the larger socio-cultural system in which we are embedded is not held responsible for its discrimination, neglect and abuse.

Buddhism

Buddhism

Dukkha, Avidya, Atman — Buddha

Monks and Laity

18: How Our World Views Keep Us Stuck in the Drama Triangle

In Buddhism, Monks, Laity and humanity are Victims of their own ignorance, creating bad karma which keeps them caught in delusion and *samsara*. Suffering, ignorance and the belief that there is a permanent self are Persecutors. The Buddha, meaning his teachings of the Four Nobel Truths and the Eightfold Noble Path, is the Rescuer.

The heavy rules of discipline for monks can be experienced either as Rescuers or Persecutors in the normal life in a monastery. To the extent that religious rules do not conform with the path of one's life compass, as reflected by one's emerging potentials, they are indeed Persecutors. Similarly, monasteries and monks are supported by the offerings of laity, who believe they are accruing good karma by doing so. However, if the concept of karma is a socially-created delusion, as noted above in the discussion of Hinduism, it is itself both Rescuer and Persecutor.

In the history of Buddhism, dependency upon support by the laity of monastic communities made it very easy for Buddhism to be destroyed within India by the Moslem invasions from the 12th to the 16th centuries. Therefore, one would have to conclude that the monastic system, while effective and supportive in times of peace and therefore functioning in the role of Rescuer, in times of social turmoil or in the milieu of contemporary Western civilization in which there is rarely a karma-based support of monasteries by the surrounding communities, monastic life loses some, much or all of its Rescuing function.

Buddhists have to be wary of the distinct possibility that their belief system makes a Persecutor of their sense of self. If there is no permanent self, as Buddhists believe, then the belief that one is a self creates a direct conflict with one's religious doctrines. Reality, that is, the moment to moment experience that there is a self, becomes a Persecutor in relation to the Rescuing affirmation that the experience, as well as the belief that there is a real, permanent self, is a delusion.

Like Hindus, Buddhists have to be wary of turning life itself into a Persecutor. If life is *samsara* and *dukkha* or suffering, then Buddhists risk defining reality in a way that there is no practical escape from Persecution within the Drama Triangle as long as one is alive. Theoretically, one could attain nirvana and Buddhahood, but how likely is that? In the meantime, what does one do with the reality that one is a victim of *samsara*, attempting to be rescued by the Buddha, Dharma and Sangha? The goal of Nirvana itself, in that it is imagined to be an attainable state, can itself be a Persecutor, because enlightenment is a forever unfolding process rather than a goal or destination that can be attained once and for all.

18: How Our World Views Keep Us Stuck in the Drama Triangle

The Chinese World View

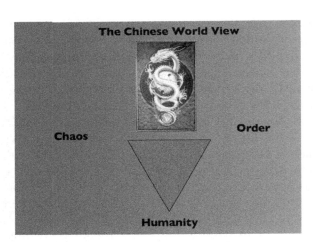

One cannot speak about "Chinese Religion" because Mandarin doesn't contain a word for "religion." What we call religion is so engrained in Chinese culture and society that it is not differentiated from them. As such, it provides an excellent example of a world view that is so pervasive that it is essentially invisible to those who hold it.

China has a longer history of devastating floods, earthquakes and invasions than any other civilization and this has severely affected the development of its world view. In 1887, 1931 and 1938 there was a series of devastating floods of the Yellow River, the country's second longest river. The 1887 flood of the Yellow River in Henan, China killed over 900,000 and flooded over 50,000 sq. miles. Estimates of the total death toll range from 145,000 to between 3.7 million and 4 million. In the 1930s, floods throughout huge tracts of China killed more than 400,000 people. These three floods collectively killed millions and are considered to be the three deadliest floods in history and among the most destructive natural disasters ever recorded. They are almost certainly the deadliest of the 20th century. Compare these floods to the worst flood in US history, the 1927 Mississippi River flood that killed 500. It pales in significance in comparison to even the smallest of the floods in China mentioned above.

The Chinese have more than one great flood myth, the most common being the Gun-Yu myth, during the reign of Emperor Yao, approximately 2300 BC. What is

18: How Our World Views Keep Us Stuck in the Drama Triangle

interesting about Great Flood stories in Chinese mythology is that in distinction to all other flood myths found throughout the world, they are not considered a punishment from an almighty being for disobedience but were thought to be the result of natural causes. For the Chinese, nature is both the Persecutor and the Rescuer, not the gods.

Equally horrendous in their devastation and impact upon the Chinese psyche has been a long history of cataclysmic earthquakes. In 1290 in Chihli a 6.8 earthquake killed about 100,000; in 1303 in Hongdong, an 8.0 tremor killed 200,000 and two cities, Taiyuan and Pingyang were leveled. The 1556 Shaanxi earthquake at 8.0 and killing 830,000 is the deadliest earthquake of all time. The 1668 quake in Tancheng at 8.0 killed more than 50,000; In 1695 the Linfen tremor at 7.8 killed 52,600; the 1718 Tongwei-Gansu earthquake at 7.5 killed 75,000; the 1786 Sichuan tremor at 7.75 killed more than 100,000; the 1879 Gansu earthquake at 8.0 killed 22,000; the 1920 Haiyuan quake at 7.8 killed 234,117 and is the 4th deadliest earthquake of all time. The 1976 Tangshan tremor at 7.5 killed 242,419 and is the 3rd deadliest of all time. The 2008 Sichuan quake at 7.9 killed 68,712 with more than 18,392 missing and 4.8 million people rendered homeless. Compare these earthquakes with the most destructive in US history, the 8.2 1906 San Francisco earthquake that killed 7,000.

As if horrendous floods and earthquakes did not generate enough chronic social vulnerability and anxiety, China has had to live with repeated invasions throughout its history. This is because it has no natural barriers on its northern, western or southern borders. For over 2,000 years nomadic people to the north and west of China regularly harassed, invaded and even conquered the settled agricultural civilizations of the Chinese Empire. Some were formidable enough to conquer and rule the entirety of China. Many of these invasions lasted hundreds of years, with entire foreign ruling dynasties set up by invaders. The Mongol Yuan dynasty lasted from 1279 to 1368; the Manchu Qing dynasty lasted from 1662 to 1911. As a result, for over 2,000 years, successive Chinese emperors were preoccupied with containing their northern neighbors and expended vast amounts of resources to build walls to keep out the invaders.

China was invaded in 763 by Tibetans, by the Jin dynasty and Mongols in the 11 and 1200's, Manchurians in the 1600's, in 1839 by the United Kingdom, in 1856 by a French-British Alliance, in 1894 by Japan, in 1900 by the United Kingdom, Russia, Japan, the US, France, Germany, Italy and Austria-Hungary, in 1937 and 1939 by Japan. Compare this history to that of the US, which has never been ruled by another country and the capital, Washington DC, has only been invaded once, by the British, in 1814, for a period of 26 hours.

More than most other countries in world history, China has been a victim of natural disasters and major invasions. Americans have no collective conception of the epic nature of these repeated disasters. The major Persecutor in traditional Chinese consciousness are therefore not Gods or men but chaos, disharmony and imbalances among natural forces. A major concept in the Chinese world view is luck, chance or fate.

In Chinese folk shamanism, Taoism and Buddhism, forgotten, disrespected or vengeful ghosts are Persecutors. Offerings of various sorts and supplications to friendly ghosts provide rescuing. Offerings are shows of respect, and respect runs very deep indeed in Chinese consciousness, reaching its full expression as early as 400 BC in the thought of Master K'ung, known in the West as Confucius. Propriety, demonstrated by the respectful maintenance of familial and social roles, is the major rescuer from chaos, disharmony and disrespect for Chinese culture. Clearly, the Chinese have had to learn that they cannot control nature but they can relate to it and interact with it through respect. This is another fundamental and profound way that the Chinese world view differs from other traditions. Respect for nature has generalized into society, with interpersonal respect for individuals according to their social roles as fundamental to the functioning of society and personal development. To this day, good luck remains a powerful Rescuer in the Chinese mentality while bad luck is a powerful Persecutor. Since luck is by nature whimsical and nearly chaotic, it can only be influenced. Consequently, it is another manifestation of the Chinese experience of being subject to the preferences of natural forces that remain largely outside human control.

Interestingly, rather than using natural catastrophes and invasions to justify chronic Victim status, the Chinese world view focuses on equal parts self-reliance within socially-proscribed roles and collective interdependence. Perhaps because of the constant threat of uncontrollable natural disasters and invasions, the Chinese world view tends to be intensely pragmatic and industrious.

Judaism

18: How Our World Views Keep Us Stuck in the Drama Triangle

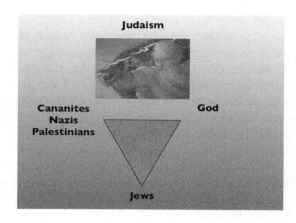

Judaism attempts to control reality by making a deal with it. Jews agree to obey God and God rewards them by giving them priority. They are privileged in His eyes, are favored and possess an exclusivity and exceptionalism absent for others.

Judaism has also done an excellent job of maintaining social cohesion by using a number of clever ploys. The first is to proclaim the requirements and preferences of priests and leaders as the voice of God: "God said." The benefit of this strategy is that believers are much more likely to be impressed, respectful and even obey an injunction, law or commandment that they believe is uttered by deity than they are if the same information is stated by a mere human. God then not only rescues his people by the promulgation of sacred law, but rescues the priesthood and leaders by generating considerable obedience in the populace.

Secondly, powerful ethnic bonds create a cultural "Jewish" identity that is stronger than most national identities. Jews are brought up to first be Jews and secondly citizens, parents or children. Loyalty to the clan comes first, and that loyalty is sacred, because loyalty to Judaism is loyalty to God.

Disobedience is controlled by teachings emphasizing sin and guilt, thereby generating strong self-control via conscience. However, this tool of religious cohesion is softening somewhat as Jews in the diaspora come in contact with individuals and world views that are not based on clan allegiance.

A third basic factor that is highly effective in maintaining social cohesion within Judaism is the inculcation and maintenance of chronic victim status. Jews are raised to see themselves as victims, and the history of Biblical, Middle Age and holocaust persecutions are reinforced again and again as terrible collective tragedies visited upon innocent Jews by vicious persecuting non-Jews. The message is that Jews are victims, that non-Jews cannot be trusted, and that Jews must therefore stick together to protect each other. This belief system has the powerful psychological benefit of increasing group cohesion, since no one wants to feel like they have let down other members of their clan.

This loyalty to the clan in the face of a myth of constant victimization causes even atheistic Jews to support apartheid Israel as a hedge against some future possible pogrom. In that model, Israel replaces God as Rescuer and Goyim, that is, non-Jews, become the Persecutors. The power of cultural scripting in the family, in the synagogue and in Jewish schools is not to be underestimated, and in Israel Judaism has become more rigid and exclusivistic than ever, with most Israeli Jews endorsing right-wing zionist political and spiritual leaders.

In the back of most Jews' minds is that they need to support each other and Israel, no matter how corrupt individual Jews or Israel might become, because there could always be that next persecution when they are going to need help and refuge. Jews who question their victim status or the cultural Victim status of Judaism by pointing out inconvenient truths like the bloody Hebraic conquest of Canaan or the current Jewish treatment of Palestinians and Moslems, are likely to labeled a "self-hating Jew."

Chronic victim status is perhaps the most powerful position in the Drama Triangle because Victims are blameless and therefore cannot be held accountable nor expected to be responsible in the same way that non-Jews, that is, Persecutors, are expected to be. Confirmed Victims can also self-righteously persecute without losing their status as victims, because in their own minds they are only acting in self-defense, regardless of how obviously and completely they are abusing the human rights of others.

Judaism has therefore created a particularly toxic version of the Drama Triangle. Not only are all Goyim potential Persecutors, but Jews are self-identified as Victims. Resenting this, due to the helplessness and powerlessness that Victim status entails, any and all forms of persecution thereby become justified. Jews are allowed to see themselves and other Jews as Victims, and Gentiles are allowed to see Jews as Victims as long as that translates into special treatment and rights, but at the same time Jews resent being treated as or being viewed as Victims in other circumstances because, although this is strenuously denied by Jews, their status as The Chosen People defines a self-image that says, "I'm better than you." Jewish self-rescuing includes taking what is not theirs (other people's lands, possessions and lives), but more importantly, reliance upon their special status with God to justify discrimination against non-Jews and demands for special treatment and rights not provided by Jews to non-Jewish residents of Israel or the West Bank.

Christianity

*18: How Our World Views Keep Us Stuck
in the Drama Triangle*

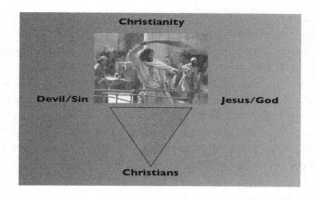

Like all world religions, Christianity is convinced that it is the One True Religion and that those who believe in the Christian God and his Son will have life everlasting while others, not so much. If non-Christians are lucky they will spend eternity in some limbo-like purgatory; if they are unlucky, some level of Dante's Inferno awaits them. God and Jesus rescue all believers from sin and the devil. While good works help, what is important are beliefs that most branches of Christianity spell out in a doxology that believers repeat whenever they go to church services.

However, not even Christians are ensured freedom from the fires of Hell, since their sins could put them there, even though they are Christians. This is important, because fear of damnation is a central tool by which Christianity has traditionally ensured compliance by the laity, This has been combined with strong teachings regarding sin and guilt which Christians internalize as conscience, generating self-monitoring and compliance with Church law.

Although Christianity is entered around a belief in divine love, compassion and grace, exclusivity and superiority show themselves in centuries of Church-sanctioned persecution of both other Christian sects and non-believers. While all Christians believe they know who the "real historical Jesus" was and what "real" Christianity is, as opposed to the "false doctrines" taught by other Christian sects and non-Christians, they generally remain blind to the many ways in which they remain trapped in the Drama Triangle.

The consequence is growth of Christianity among the relative illiterate. For example, Christian missionary work has been most successful over the last one hundred years in Africa and other parts of the Third World. At the same time, Christianity has experienced diminishing numbers and influence among the highly educated, particularly in Europe and the United States, for whom blind faith and belief "just because" is no longer sufficient. Without the strong glue of karma

18: How Our World Views Keep Us Stuck in the Drama Triangle

used by Hinduism and Buddhism, Christianity, like Judaism and Islam, has had to largely resort to fear of punishment by God and His Church and to the inculcation of guilt through the creation of an overactive, psychological unhealthy conscience. The result is that the role of Persecutor has loomed over the history of Christianity, with the stick of eternal punishment as great a factor for compliance as the carrot of salvation. The problem is that popular culture generally glorifies what used to be called sin and people observe no punishment for those who indulge in activities that are against the teachings of the Church. When role models, such as priests pay no attention to the proscriptions of Christianity, for instance with pedophilia, why should the laity?

Christianity maintains a sick and twisted relationship with Judaism. In that Christianity sprang from Judaism and Jesus himself was a Jew and Rabbi, Christians feel a special historical affinity with Jews, seeing them as worshiping the same God. In fact, in mainstream Christian apocalyptic mythology, the Jews must first regain control of the Holy Land before Jesus will return. At that time Jews will recognize Jesus as their messiah or be destroyed. Judaism has used this mythology to gain surprising support from many Christians for its Zionistic, colonialistic, imperialistic and apartheid policies and actions directed toward Palestinians and arabs. It has also done an excellent job at convincing the majority of American Christians that Islam preaches terrorism and that therefore Christians should be afraid of Moslems and support Israel in its persecution of Palestinians, Arabs and Moslems.

At the same time many Christians still hold the view of the Gospel of St. Matthew, that Jews and Judaism are responsible for the death and crucifixion of Jesus and therefore view Jews and Judaism as Persecutors. However, at the same time Christians feel guilt, which is shown by their excusing or supporting Jewish theft and atrocities carried out against Palestinians, Arabs and Moslems, regarding their historical anti-semitism.

Because there is no salvation within the Drama Triangle and because Christianity, like other world religions, is based on and an expression of the Drama Triangle, its long-term existence is unlikely. To maintain credibility it has to morph into a world view that is not based on the Drama Triangle. But this is so far from its historical roots and self-definition that this appears to be highly unlikely.

Islam

18: How Our World Views Keep Us Stuck in the Drama Triangle

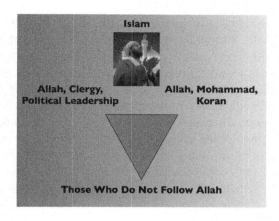

Obedience is basic to Islam. You obey the Koran and you are rescued by Allah; disobey and you will be punished. Islam is essentially a religion of service and kindness; it has been viciously and consciously portrayed as an intolerant, murderous religion by zionistic Jews who want the help of the world in fracturing the Arab nations that surround Israel. Christians have accepted this view, partially out of fraternal affinity with "the People of the Book," partially for guilt for centuries of participating in or turning a blind eye to the persecution of Jews and partially out of fear of Islam, which is largely not understood or misunderstood by Westerners. In addition, both neoliberals and neoconservatives in the West have made a great deal of money from selling arms to kill Arabs and Moslems, whether by the West, Israel, or to other Arabs and Moslems.

Until the fall of 2015, when Russia intervened in Syria, this strategy of first demonizing Arabs, arming jihadis and bombing Moslems in multiple countries, was largely successful, with Obama and NATO bombing seven Moslem countries over the course of his administration. However, most Moslems view Wahhabism, extreme jihadist Islam issuing out of Saudi Arabia, as wrong, evil and not a true expression of the teachings of the Prophet. It produces a Persecuting caricature of the intentions of the Koran which the above-aligned forces are all too eager to exaggerate.

Even with the best of interpretations, like Judaism, Christianity and Hinduism, Islam does indeed advocate violence. Islam also functions within the Drama Triangle for basically the same reasons that it does within the other Western monotheisms. Guilt does not seem to play as important a role as adherence to the laws of its strict patriarchy. These maintain social order and identity and perhaps more than Christianity and diasphoric Judaism mainstream Islam punishes non-conformity to religious law or sharia. However, much the same standard appears to still be operative within orthodox Judaism. Like all other religions, most Moslems function well within the context of their religious faith because they live and work within a religious collective that mutually supports those who share the same beliefs and world view. All religions function adequately and are supportive of growth within the bubble of their own suppositions; it is only when those suppositions or fundamental assumptions come in conflict with different world views that operate on conflicting assumptions that it begins to dawn on believers that they are indeed functioning within the Drama Triangle.

This is occurring today for many Muslims as they come into contact with other world views and recognize that the intensely paternalistic structure of Islam not only cuts them off from many global opportunities for growth but keeps them stuck in the Drama Triangle.

Atheism

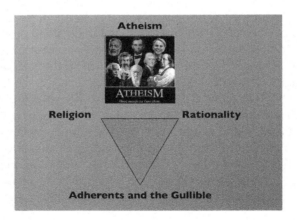

While atheists tend to put themselves outside the Drama Triangle by viewing themselves neither as adherents or gullible, they are indeed adherents of rationality, viewing religion as either irrelevant or as a Persecutor. Reason and accurate information are their Rescuers. This perceptual framework does indeed place atheists inside the Drama Triangle. While not a religion, atheism causes its adherents to remain caught in the same underlying dynamics that religionists are.

18: How Our World Views Keep Us Stuck in the Drama Triangle

Richard Dawkins provides an excellent example of same: "Revealed faith is not harmless nonsense, it can be lethally dangerous nonsense." (A dangerous Persecutor.) "Dangerous because it gives people unshakeable confidence in their own righteousness." (The self-righteousness of the Persecutor role.) "Dangerous because it gives them false courage to kill themselves, which automatically removes normal barriers to killing others. Dangerous because it teaches enmity to others labelled only by a difference of inherited tradition." (Persecution based on a sense of moral superiority,) "And dangerous because we have all bought into a weird respect, which uniquely protects religion from normal criticism." (We rescue believers from the persecution of their own delusions.) These are characteristics of the Persecutor in the Drama Triangle.

Dawkins continues: "An atheist is just somebody who feels about Yahweh the way any decent Christian feels about Thor or Baal or the golden calf. As has been said before, we are all atheists about most of the gods that humanity has ever believed in. Some of us just go one god further." By this statement Dawkins is pointing out that atheists are not as deeply enmeshed in the Drama Triangle as religionists, in that they do not look for rescue from supernatural forces. This is true, but it fails to recognize ways that atheists remain within their own version of the Drama Triangle.

Atheists see themselves as Victims to the extent that they feel persecuted by religious culture that they think is a danger to them, their families, lifestyles and culture. Atheists also tend to view the young and gullible as Victims of religious myth and teachings. Some atheists, like Dawkins, put themselves into the role of Rescuer by taking upon themselves the mission of "saving" others from the irrationality and destructiveness of religious beliefs.

Atheists are indeed in a position of relative objectivity in relationship to the prepersonal, pre-rational versions of the Drama Triangle espoused by religious believers. However, they typically confuse disassociation with prepersonal versions of the Drama Triangle with separation from it, not realizing that versions can and do exist in the personal, rational bands of human development. The same can be said about agnostics, who are in yet a more objectified position than atheists. This is because agnostics suspend both belief and disbelief in deities and often religion. However, this does not mean that agnostics are not strongly invested in self-rescuing or persecution by other, non-religious beliefs, such as human rights, scientific humanism or systems of political, business and familial governance.

Scientific Humanism

18: How Our World Views Keep Us Stuck in the Drama Triangle

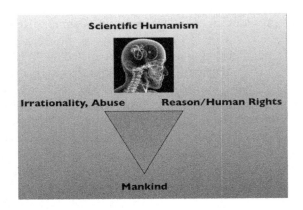

Scientific humanism is different from atheism because it may or may not put itself in opposition to religion. Throughly secular, scientific humanism generally believes in a religion called "human progress." The major rescuing religious rite is called "empiricism," or the consensus validation of results of experiments that claim to show results above chance. Scientific humanism is also different from atheism in that it is a strong advocate for human rights.

Scientific humanism is in the role of Persecutor in that it tends to be reductionist, that is, it reduces aspects of experience that are not observable or repeatable to prepersonal phenomena. For example, scientific humanists tend to view drug or meditation-induced mystical experiences as prepersonal decompensation, to be controlled with medication. However, medication can disrupt the ability of the body and mind to integrate the experience on its own and result in a missed opportunity for major growth.

Scientific humanists tend to be Victims of their own self-assurance that they have things figured out because they are rational and humanistic, caring about others, animals and the planet. Indeed, scientific humanism is a much milder form of the Drama Triangle than religion provides, but misery is relative. The depths of delusion and suffering can, relatively speaking, be as profound for a scientific humanist as they can be for a religious adherent.

New Age

*18: How Our World Views Keep Us Stuck
in the Drama Triangle*

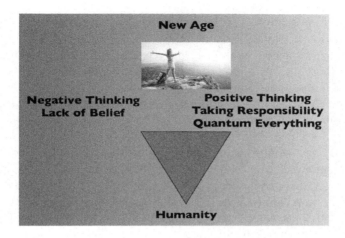

New Age has core beliefs which, when accepted, tend to put adherents in the role of self-rescuers and Rescuers of others. Positive thinking, an American tradition that can be traced back a t least least to Ralph Waldo Emerson in the 1800's, assumes that you create your reality by how you think. Therefore, you can create the reality you want if you only think positive thoughts and banish all negative ones from your awareness. The implication is that non-positive thinking is a Persecutor, to be identified and overcome.

Positivity in thought, feeling and action are excellent when they are grounded in reason and, beyond that, in the priorities of your life compass. However, when most positivity is examined, it is not. Instead, it is grounded in pre-rational beliefs ("Every day in every way I am getting better and better") and our own limited priorities, which we are convinced reflect our conscience, intuition or the will of God. How do we know? And if so, are these sources the same as the priorities of our life compass? How do we know?

New Age spirituality is also in alignment with much contemporary psychology in that it assumes that you are responsible for your reality. Dream characters are for this belief system self-aspects; if you are unhappy, awake or dreaming, you created your unhappiness. Consequently, many New Age believers embrace the concept of karma, because it gives a spiritual explanation and justification for the endless grandiosity of taking responsibility for whatever one experiences.

How taking responsibility for everything you experienced has been explained above in regard to karma and Hinduism, but to relate it more specifically to New Age thinking, the problem is not only that it makes you much more powerful than you actually are, but it deprives others of their responsibility. If you are fired you may be able to deal with your shock and fear by owning it, but what about the responsibility of your employer? Do they have no accountability for their actions? In addition, taking complete responsibility is essentially solipsistic. It validates psychological geocentrism, which keeps you stuck in prepersonal or personal levels of development; you aren't going to outgrow your addiction to your belief that you are somebody as long as you hold some self responsible for everything you experience. What about the autonomy of the "other," whether people, objects or dream characters? How respectful is it to deny the same authentic otherness to the objects of your experience that you expect to be given to you?

When people are young or immature, world views that encourage taking responsibility such as karma and positive thinking can indeed be important and helpful. However, as people learn that lesson and continue to develop, other lessons become more important. To continue to emphasize taking responsibility when one already has a tendency to take too much is going to block further development. Somewhere during mid-personal it becomes important to start questioning the dogma of perpetual responsibility.

A third major rescuing component of New Age belief systems is scientism. By this IDL means the tendency of New Age to cloak its belief system in a thin, plastic, pseudo-scientific veneer by offering explanations for mind, thoughts, emotions and the interdependence of life in terms of energy, fields, and quantum everything. If I can sound scientific enough perhaps you will think that science actually backs up what I say and therefore I will gain credibility in your eyes. You are more likely to give my ideas about positivity and responsibility validity because after all, I use scientific jargon.

Here is a good example of the use of scientific jargon to make a bioresonance device of unproven ability, sound "scientific:" ""The 'Oberon' diagnostic telemetric data processing apparatus for nonlinear analysis is designed to assess the condition of an organism, perform dynamic monitoring of the condition of homeostasis, and forecast the stages of treatment and the development of complications. From the physical point of view the apparatus is a system of electronic oscillators resonating on the wavelengths of the electromagnetic radiation whose energy is proportionate to the energy of disruption of the predominant bonds supporting the structural organization of the object. Information about the condition of the organs is taken without contact with the aid of a flip-flop sensor collecting the barely perceptible fluctuations of signals isolated from the statistical average noise characteristics of the fields and transformed into a digital sequence, and processed by a microprocessor for transmission to the computer through an interface cable."[8]

It is difficult to find anyone in the New Age movement who does not appeal to science to validate their particular form of metaphysics. By "metaphysic" I mean

---

8   http://humanism.al.ru/en/articles.phtml?num=000013

18: How Our World Views Keep Us Stuck
in the Drama Triangle

any pre-rational belief system. Most of these people have no training in science and particularly the fields that they allude to, such as quantum physics, yet they speak as if they were authorities. Why? Put quantum anything in the title and you get attention. Quantum consciousness! Quantum leaps! Quantum mechanics! Quantum coffee! (Yes, it really exists...) Quantum workplaces! Quantum health! Quantum chess! Unfortunately, I could not find either Quantum toads or Quantum Gummy Bears, but Quantum spirituality? Definitely!

A fourth major rescuing aspect of New Age involves its inability to grasp the difference between placebo cures that work no better than chance and empirically-tested treatments. This alone demonstrates that New Age is a prepersonal and pre-rational mentality that is convinced it is integral and transpersonal. New Age insists that pre-scientific systems like homeopathy, reiki, astrology and crystal healing be given the same amount of credibility as penicillin, electro-cardiograms, biofeedback, and cognitive behavioral therapy.

New Age uses a late personal egalitarian and pluralistic world view to imagine that it transcends and includes rational science when it still refuses to accept the standards of empiricism. New Age wants to maintain its belief system that the mind can cure anything and that therefore any treatment that the mind believes in can and will work. The amazing powers of the mind are the Rescuer from physical and mental illness as well as life problems of all sorts. Most coaching falls into this category of New Age pre-rational world view.

There is a fifth self-rescuing aspect of New Age which is endemic and very basic. New Age is, like almost all belief systems addressed here, profoundly elevationistic. It assumes it is transpersonal when it is actually functioning at prepersonal or at best an early personal developmental level with a thin rational overlay. There are very simple tests to determine if this is the case. When you examine the beliefs that are fundamental to a particular world view, are they supported by reason or by pre-rational appeals? Examples of the latter are appeals to scripture, authorities, anecdotal accounts, miracles, mythologies, psychically-derived information or channelings. While such sources have their uses and validity, they do not rise to rational level validity because they are notoriously difficult to verify by repetition or a consensus of observers broader than the community of believers. Why is this important?

According to integral, as we shall see below, every level of development includes and transcends all previous levels. If you think you are at a high level but it does not include some lower level, your default assumption needs to be that you are mistaken, that your development is actually at a lower level. This is the case with New Age because belief in positivity and personal responsibility, to the degree taken by New Age, is pre-rational; it is not based on reason due to the factors mentioned above. Without reason, in this case subjecting your belief

18: How Our World Views Keep Us Stuck in the Drama Triangle

system to the tests of empiricism, you can have temporary trans-rational states but you cannot have ongoing, maintained trans-rational and transpersonal levels of development. Therefore, to think that you have attained some transpersonal level when your beliefs are pre-rational, as is the case with the vast majority of New Age, is elevationism.

The assumption of New Age that some thoughts are Persecutors is in contradistinction to IDL, which views negative thinking, feeling and life events as wake-up calls to be listened to, respected, and learned from. The assumption is that only by doing so can the intentions behind "negativity" be reincorporated into a broader, more powerful and freer sense of self.

By all means, continue to hold those New Age beliefs and practices that are important to you. Simply do so in the awareness that these are most likely prepersonal and pre-rational beliefs and practices which are subject to prepersonal and pre-rational versions of the Drama Triangle. That does not make them wrong, bad or not useful; it simply means that they are neither rational, much less trans-rational. Accept and use them for what they are and do not attempt to make them into something they are not.

Integral

Integral psychology, philosophy and spirituality are most closely associated with the AQAL model of Ken Wilber, which stands for "All levels, states, quadrants, types and lines." *Levels* of development are prepersonal, personal and transpersonal, with each having an early, middle and late stage. There is also a transitional stage between personal and transpersonal called "vision-logic" and a

18: How Our World Views Keep Us Stuck in the Drama Triangle

"non-stage stage," the non-dual, after late transpersonal. While stages are permanent, stable, successive structures, each of which includes and transcends previous developmental stages, *states* are temporary and may either be natural, such as waking, dreaming and deep sleep, or extraordinary, such as drug, mystical and near death experiences.

What has just been said about New Age regarding elevationism unfortunately applies to Integral as well. People often assume that because they have had an expansive state experience that they must have arrived at some high level of development, but this is a mistake; children and criminals can have near death, psychic and mystical experiences. *Quadrants* refer to the co-evolving dimensions of interpersonal and individual behavior, values and interior consciousness. *Types* refers to the "style" of development, which may be more "masculine" or "feminine." There are some four basic *lines*, cognitive, self, moral and relationship, with some twenty others, including proprioceptive or bodily awareness, seen in athletes, as well as musical, artistic and mathematical lines.

The cognitive line leads, which means that you cannot develop into a level or a capability that you do not already perceive or conceptualize in some way. Your world view has to conceive of some level of development for you to perceive it. The problem is that people who learn the integral cognitive model often mistake cognitive comprehension of an integral world view, which is an advancement on the cognitive *line*, the leading line, with *stage* development; they think that because they can *conceive* transpersonal realities that they have therefore attained some stable integral level of development, vision-logic or beyond, when in fact they have merely advanced in their cognitive line.

This is the basic elevationistic delusion of integral and one profound example involves the many people who viewed themselves as integral and "cutting edge evolutionaries"[9] who endorsed Hillary Clinton, a candidate for US President. These "evolutionaries" did so essentially for issues of identity politics. Because people at late personal or later cognitive line development embrace egalitarianism and pluralism, they are repulsed by Trump's xenophobia, misogyny, racism, lying and general crudity. However, Clinton not only had a track record as a murderess (she personally ordered drone attacks that assassinated men, women and children in contradistinction to US and international law) but as corrupt within the context of public office. Donald Trump had no previous history of murder. Because it is not rational to advocate for a killer over a non-killer as President, the strong implication is that these self-styled "integral evolutionaries" have not yet advanced in their overall development to mid-personal, which makes decisions based on rationality. Instead, they possess a center of development that is at best early personal, but with strong cognitive and interpersonal lines that mask their

---

9 https://www.change.org/p/robby-mook-evolutionaries-for-hillary-clinton

18: How Our World Views Keep Us Stuck in the Drama Triangle

developmental deficits.

How could this happen? Integral tends to chronically over-estimate developmental level, in a process called "elevationism," and presents itself in such a way that Integral adherents tend to do so as well. This makes people feel good and gains more people to Integral because adherents get to feel they are one of the "few elect," one of the "5% of the population that has reached "2nd Tier."

The problem lies in how we determine our actual level of development using Integral. Instead of associating both the self line and overall development with the leading cognitive line, that is, our grasp of AQAL, a much more realistic and authentic criteria would be to identify our lagging or fixated line or lines. This is easy to do by finding out what we do and who we become when we have a "melt-down," when life goes south and stays south. Your authentic center of gravity, your genuine center of development, is likely to be one stage above your most wounded major line, at best, meaning that for almost all of us our actual level of development is late prepersonal or early personal, with strong interpersonal, communicative and intellectual skills masking our weakest lines.

AQAL rescues people by validating that they really are special, one of the elect, because they are smart enough to understand and embrace AQAL. This saves them from persecuting ignorance – the state of unawareness of AQAL – and either reductionism, which they think they do not do but that scientists and intellectuals do, and elevationism, which they think they do not do but which religionists, some psychologists (such as Jung and Assagioli) and New Age types do. To the extent that Integral thinkers stay trapped in this delusional perceptual cognitive distortion they lack the ability to live and grow into any real integration or clarity.

A second fundamental perceptual cognitive distortion associated with Integral that tends to keep its adherents in the Drama Triangle is that its center of reference tends to be the self and self-development rather than life itself. The emphasis of Integral tends to be on how we define ourselves rather than the multiple perspectives that life itself takes. Indeed, this is appropriate, because until vision-logic, that is, until development is post-personal, development is naturally self-centered, even if the cognitive line has advanced to understand multi-perspectivalism. As a consequence, the agenda of life tends to be defined as the agenda of self by the self, although Wilber gives recognition to involution as well, which is not a priority of the self.

IDL tends to disclose this problem with Integral through its interviewing of multiple perspectives, all of which have a degree of autonomous authenticity but no permanent self-sense. This disclosure shows up as priorities that differ from those of the evolving self and which are broader and more inclusive, implying that they are more reflective of the priorities of life itself than are those currently

18: How Our World Views Keep Us Stuck in the Drama Triangle

chosen by the self.

The reason this matters from a practical standpoint is that integral life practices, or one might say yogic disciplines, are generated by the self without consideration as to whether these goals and practices are in alignment with the priorities of life itself. One just assumes so, on the basis of authority, prevailing cultural memes or "intuition." In order to evolve beyond a self-centered reality we have to have some methodology, like IDL, that allows us to compare our priorities with those o f emerging potentials, of priorities and goals that are attempting to be born within us but which include yet transcend not only our own goals but who we think we are – our self line.

This confusion keeps us victimized through a limited and separated self-definition that insists on "running the show," setting life goals and making important decisions. While these are indeed core responsibilities of the self, the intention for IDL is for goals to be set in coordination with the priorities of life rather than independently. A self-centered definition of reality, something that Integral continues to represent in all three of the transpersonal developmental stages, is a form of self-rescuing, maintaining what Wilber very well recognizes as the Atman Project. This self then becomes our Persecutor, showing up in the transpersonal realms as yogic, saintly and sage dysfunctions.[10]

All of this implies that no real level of the transpersonal has been achieved, but instead the self has experienced one or more state openings into transpersonal perspectives and then assumes that the self is stable on those levels of development, when in fact the overall development is at a much lower level. This is elevationism. These dysfunctions largely manifest because the intermediate steps have not been climbed by the lagging or fixated lines, generally of self, morality and/or empathy.

Therefore. claims of transpersonal development by Integral are rarely authentic, as can be validated by investigation of the life of any guru or enlightened master for which we have a reasonably thorough historical record. What we have instead are temporary state breakthroughs imagined to be stable self-line attainment of this or that transpersonal level of development. But many of these "spiritual masters" or mystical or near death experiencers do not even possess an Integral cognitive model, so how could their transpersonal openings be integral anything?

The consequences of all this are not pretty for Integral. Those who over-estimate their developmental level (who doesn't?) set themselves up as elitists who lose all credibility when the mask is ripped off. We have experienced a major cultural earthquake with the establishment, neocons, neoliberals in the UK, the US and the EU having to realize that the "deplorables" prefer uncertainty and liars

---

10 Wilber, K. *Transformations of Consciousness: Conventional and Contemplative Perspectives on Development* (co-authors: Jack Engler, Daniel Brown), 1986.

18: How Our World Views Keep Us Stuck in the Drama Triangle

they can relate to over the certainty of corruption and hypocrisy provided by elitist liars. We have seen the same thing in the loss of credibility of almost all spiritual gurus, when their lives can be observed and they can be held accountable for the contradictions in them, from Chogyam Tungpa, Adi da, Andrew Cohen, Genpo Roshi, Robert Masters, Marc Gafni to Ken Wilber.

Those who embrace Integral can avoid problems that land them in the Drama Triangle by interviewing multiple alternative perspectives that include but transcend their own and follow those recommendations that meet the test of triangulation, that is, represent a consensus of high scoring interviewed emerging potentials, that also meet with no blocking objections from respected waking authorities, and that agree with their own common sense.

Meditation

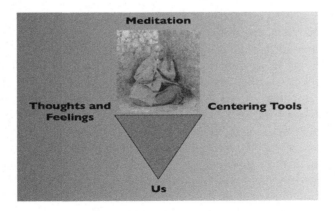

Most meditation is done from within the Drama Triangle. However, that neither indicates that it is a mistake to meditate or that it is better not to meditate. On the contrary, an understanding of the Drama Triangle merely provides another context in which to approach meditation. We can then ask, "How can I minimize the Drama Triangle during this period of meditation?"

Assume that meditation itself is a form of self-rescuing. While on a practical

*18: How Our World Views Keep Us Stuck
in the Drama Triangle*

level, it is rescuing from one or more of the five *skandhas,* our thoughts, feelings, images, sensations and consciousness; more fundamentally, it involves rescuing ourselves from any self-sense whatsoever.

Generally, self-rescuing in meditation will be framed in other ways: as experiencing God's grace, returning to some state of oneness experienced in a previous meditation, mystical or near death experiences, burning off negative karma, aligning the chakras and raising the kundalini, earning the right to be reborn in more desirable circumstances, transcending *samsara* and accessing *moksha* or freedom, escaping *dukkha* or suffering, attaining nirvana. The reasons and formulations are endless. In any case, it is wise to identify you own by asking yourself, "Why do I meditate?" "What are the reasons I give myself for my practice?" List them. Then decide for yourself, "To what extent are these forms of self-rescuing?" You decide.

From the above it is clear that escape from persecution provides part of the motivation for much meditation. We want to develop objectivity toward our physical and emotional pains and traumas; to escape sadness and anxiety and have less imbalance and confusion, powerlessness and helplessness. The implication is that we are Victims of such experiences. Victims seek Rescuers while putting themselves in conflict with those parts of themselves they perceive as victimizing or Persecutors.

Much of what people call "meditation" is better called imagery, contemplation, repetition, exploration, pranayama or even repression. People call these things meditation either because they don't know the difference or want the self-rescuing from real meditation that these experiences provide. Just as the idea of a life without drama feels lifeless, dull and boring to those who are addicted to the Drama Triangle, so a meditation without thoughts or feelings feels punishing and meaningless to those addicted to their thoughts and feelings. Therefore, approaches that use imagery, contemplation, repetition, exploration or repression are helpful forms of self-rescuing that can be positively viewed as intermediate steps providing "transitional objects," like binkies and teddy bears are for young children, for us as we transition to states of greater clarity and broader objectivity.

The longer you sit in meditation the more likely it becomes that awarenesses will come up that you experience as Persecutors, such as physical pains, obsessive thoughts, persistent feelings, images you can't get rid of, or outside noises that irritate you. For beginning meditators this may only take thirty seconds; for advanced meditators it may take two to four hours, but the issue is the same: sooner or later there will arise for everyone some Persecutor, and the longer you practice the more intense these persecuting interferences are likely to become.

As soon as this occurs you will want to do something to rescue yourself: repeat a mantra, repress the persecution or stop meditating entirely. Honor such feelings and actions! Do not give perceived Persecutors even greater reality by fighting with them or by feeling defeated or controlled by them. Instead, cultivate cosmic humor and smile at the tragi-comedy of your human predicament, learn from it and use the experience to do better next time. Approach your meditation periods as a game you are playing with yourself that involves not taking yourself so seriously, including those things that compose your sense of self – your sensations, feelings, images, thoughts or core identity. See Persecutors as wake-up calls and honor them without indulging them. That means name them and then move on to name what arises next in your awareness. The more lightly you hold whatever you experience the easier it will be for you to integrate and transcend whatever comes up.

The larger goal of this game is to maintain meditative clarity, with a manifestation of the values and characteristics associated with the seven octaves of IDL pranayama, throughout your everyday secular, mundane awareness. It is also to be able to maintain that awareness in your dreams, including being able to move into meditative clarity at will, whether or not you actually sit down and meditate as well as both in or out of lucid dreaming. In this sense, meditation is meant to be a period of focused cultivation of both objectivity and the various characteristics of emerging potentials. These characteristics are then meant to be generalized into your everyday awareness until there is no longer any difference between clear awareness during sitting meditation and your everyday state while washing dishes, bathing, talking to friends and family, or working.

To escape the Drama Triangle when you meditate, view all sounds, pains, sensations, thoughts, feelings and images as wake-up calls to be respected by naming them. As you do so, you move on by respectfully naming the next awareness that arises in your awareness until there are pauses or spaces where nothing to name arises. This places you in a position where you are neither ignoring or indulging your experiences while using them to move you to perspectives that transcend and include both these awareness and the Drama Triangle itself.[11]

---

11 A fuller description of "naming" as a meditation tool can be found in Dillard, J. *Waking Up.*

*18: How Our World Views Keep Us Stuck
in the Drama Triangle*

Integral Deep Listening

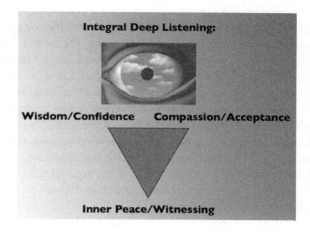

Nothing, no one, and no approach should be assumed to be free of the Drama Triangle. The common mistake is that, because we have freed ourselves of some of the most common and malicious forms of the Drama Triangle and are not aware of being in it, we assume we are, in fact, no longer enmeshed in drama. This is both a dangerous and foolish conclusion. As mentioned above, your default assumption needs to be that you are indeed stuck right now, at this moment, in the Drama Triangle, regardless of what you are doing or how far up the evolutionary ladder you have climbed, but are too deeply asleep, dreaming and sleepwalking to see it. This needs to be the default assumption for students and teachers of Integral Deep Listening as well.

In addition to the many common ways addressed elsewhere in this text, here are multiple other ways that students and teachers of IDL are prone to fall into the Drama Triangle. For example, it is quite common to discount both dreams and waking experiences as unimportant and therefore ignore them and not practice deep listening to them in an integral way. This puts both dreaming and waking experience in the role of inconsequential or annoying intrusions. They become subtle Persecutors. Students and teachers of IDL may then rescue themselves by focusing on pursuing the recommendations of previously interviewed perspectives rather than to "waste time" listening to course-correcting feedback from sources that they are sure are inconsequential and trivial. This is another form of the perceptual cognitive distortion known as psychological geocentrism.

Related to this is the common feeling among students and practitioners of IDL that they already have so many recommendations that they are either not working with or only partially successful with, that piling on even more creates feelings of overwhelm or even guilt and self-persecution. Recognize that life itself isn't judging you on whether or not you move forward on this or that recommendation; that's *your* choice and no one is telling you that you are bad or good, responsible or irresponsible for what you are to do with the recommendations that you receive. In that light, recognize that every interview is a snapshot of where you are now from some particular interviewed perspective, and that its recommendations take priority *for it* over those of previous interviews. Just be practical! If a recommendation resonates and seems to be worth your time, consider if it is feasible to make space for it in your already busy schedule.

In any case, keep a running list of who made what recommendation for what purpose. In a sense, each of these recommendations represents a prediction by a particular interviewed emerging potential. It is saying, "If you do this, I predict you will get *this* result." Acting on these recommendations is how you test the method. Do you get such results when you do?

Another trap of IDL is to confuse conceptual understanding with actual application. The point is to embody clearer states of awareness personified by interviewed emerging potentials. Application is a means to this end. Interviewed characters are much less concerned with *what* you do than *how* you do it, whether you experience your life, moment to moment, in ways that express characteristics of the seven octaves of IDL pranayama, notable in which are fearless confidence, empathy and loving kindness, wisdom, acceptance, inner peace, witnessing, abundance, joy, clear awareness, cosmic humor, trans-rationality and luminosity. Identity shifts from self or selves and specific behaviors to these qualities or characteristics, with personas and roles as useful vehicles for their manifestation but which in themselves lack *bhava,* "own being," or ontological reality.

It never hurts to ask interviewed characters, "From your perspective, am I self-rescuing? If so, how?" "Do you see me playing the Victim? If so, how?" "How do you see me Persecuting others or myself?" Their responses are never to be considered Truth, but merely to be taken under consideration. They could say you are in the Drama Triangle and be mistaken or they could say you are *not* and be mistaken. As always, rely on triangulation to reduce the depth of your self-deception.

14: How the Drama Triangle in Your Dreams Affects Your Health

    You probably work hard during the day to eat right, exercise, maintain a positive attitude, treat others with respect, not react, and generally be a good person. You can go to workshops and therapy, go to bed feeling good and still wake up feeling anxious and out of sorts. How come?
  Could it be that despite all of your excellent efforts during the day that at night while you sleep you are unconsciously undoing, undercutting, and destroying all that you have fought to create during your waking hours? If you are so sure that this is not the case, how do you know?
  Have you ever awakened anxious, irritable, or confused from a deep, dreamless sleep? Something was going on out of your awareness while you slept that created stress. Such events not only leave a physiological residue, making it harder for your body to cope with health risks; they leave a mental and emotional residue that colors your perception and affects your responsiveness, your mood, your mental focus, and your creativity. You don't have to wake up in a foul mood for this process to be taking place. It can be very subtle. Generally, the stress of unhealthy dream experiences undercut your physical, mental, and spiritual development completely out of your awareness.
    What are some of the barriers to awakening out of the Drama Triangle in Dreams? Most people give little pause to the time that they spend asleep. Our main concern is that we sleep soundly and awaken refreshed. For most of us that means deep, dreamless unconsciousness, without restlessness, interruption or awareness. As long as such a state remains our priority, any activity that prevents

14: How the Drama Triangle in Your Dreams Affects Your Health

unconsciousness is to be eliminated. As a result, we will sabotage any desire to remember our dreams or heighten our self-awareness while asleep because this will disrupt a basic habit in which we have a deep and long lasting investment. We are under enough stress already; don't we deserve a good night's sleep? Unless you are thoroughly convinced that dream recall and dream lucidity contribute in a significant way to your overall health and personal development, no amount of fascination and curiosity about dreaming is likely to make a long-term dent in this basic human desire to sink into oblivion every night.

We know that sleep is regenerative and necessary for health. Do we also know that we must be unconscious for sleep to be healthy? It seems so. A system of toxin removal from the brain has been discovered, and it is much more effective when the brain is inactive in a state of deep sleep. This has in fact been proposed as the adaptational advantage of deep sleep. How is this to be reconciled with the increased brain coherence demonstrated by regular meditators? How is it that some of these meditators can remain conscious in theta (dream) and even delta (deep) sleep?

This might best be understood as a polarity between the evolutionary movement toward objectivity, self-awareness and heightened wakefulness, on the one hand, and the involutionary movement toward subjectivity and surrender to an underlying, revitalizing, wellspring of oneness. Within sleep we have the capacity to do both, to move toward lucidity and greater wakefulness in our dreams while surrendering to involutionary subjectivity during deep sleep.[12]

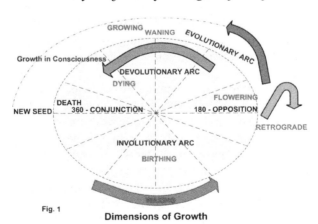

Fig. 1 **Dimensions of Growth**

If health is about being conscious of what limits the ability of life to wake up to

---

12 Diagram: Bartow, J. *Getting to Know Our Personality, Soul and Spiritual Cycles in Life*

itself within and through us as well as how to avoid those limits, then sickness is sleepwalking our way through life, pursuing limited, self-centered agendas that do not reflect the priorities of life. While such self-centered agendas are not only necessary but vital for the advancement of life's agenda in the physiosphere, that is, for plants and animals and young children, as well as into the early noosphere, into human adolescence, past that point the self-centered agendas we learn as children impede our further development if their influence is not circumscribed by growth into broader contexts.

This truth applies to the evolutionary polarity of life; the opposite appears to be true for its involutionary phase: greater health comes from surrendering all sense of self before a pervasive regression into a primordial unity. Integral approaches, such as that of Aurobindo and Wilber, as well as IDL, contend that there is a higher order synthesis of these two poles, a space in which we can be self-aware during the involution of deep sleep without interrupting the healing process and, on the other hand, experience healing unity during evolution (for example mystical and near death experiences) without thereby regressing into a state of pre-conscious dissolution. These distinctions are important; otherwise *nidra* yoga, the yoga of deep sleep wakefulness, is not healthy, nor is mystical awareness, because it is retrogression rather than progression.

Evolution is the figure or focus of life as form while involution is the ground or substrate that form returns to in winter and deep sleep. For non-manifested life, that is, life before birth and after death, when there is no self, involution is the figure or focus of life as formless creativity and luminosity, while evolution is the ground or substrate that unmanifested life returns to in spring and birth. This is not, however, to posit reincarnation in the sense of a returning self-sense. This process occurs in spectacular natural abundance in snowflakes and seeds without the need of any self-sense whatsoever.

Waking up, whether becoming more vigilant while asleep or while awake, expands your awareness of yourself beyond yourself. What was a proximal self, who you think you are, becomes a distal self, or a role or subset within a broader set or context that now defines who you are. In the evolutionary sense, waking up is about learning how to step outside of who you routinely think that you are and watching yourself go by. While the dividends for doing so are enormous, drama blocks this process.

Stepping outside of the Drama Triangle is the difference between being a more conscious participant in life, on the one hand, and, on the other, living a somnambulistic life, a victim of your own unquestioned habitual ways of thinking, feeling, and acting.

While there appear to be clear biological and psychological benefits to sleep, there is also a price to pay for going unconscious unnecessarily. First, your biochemistry controls you. Consider the basic fight or flight physiological

14: How the Drama Triangle in Your Dreams Affects Your Health

reaction to stress. Let's say you are preparing to give an important speech and you are feeling intense pressure to do a really good job. You hate public speaking and you would love to avoid giving the presentation, but you know that you can't. You know that you are going to have to put on a brave face and fight your way through it. You go to sleep feeling anxious about how you are going to do. How might this affect your ability to give your speech?

Hans Selye, the brilliant Canadian doctor and researcher, was a pioneer in research on the physical consequences of stress on organisms. He observed and described what he called the General Adaptation Syndrome, the process by which organisms adapt to stress, whether it is an illness, a death, a job loss, or an accident. When you first experience a stress you go into an alarm reaction. A cascade of powerful hormones is pumped out of your endocrine glands to alert and activate your body to deal with danger. Your heart speeds up, your breathing becomes faster and more shallow. Blood flows away from your internal organs and to your skeletal muscles to prepare you to fight or run. Your pupils constrict. If the threat does not go away as a result of all these measures, you next go into an adaptive phase in which you conserve your resources for a drawn-out defense against the attack. When you have a major life stress, such as a public speaking phobia, you can recognize both the initial alarm reaction and the secondary adaptive phase when your anxiety does not go away. Finally, if the threat remains present, something that happens with physiological stressors like drowning or running from a bear, but not from social threats like public speaking, you enter the exhaustion phase. At this point new energy is poured into your body in a last-ditch attempt to overcome the challenge; you look like you are rallying when in fact you are making a total expenditure of all your resources in one final effort to turn the tide. If this does not work, you will die.

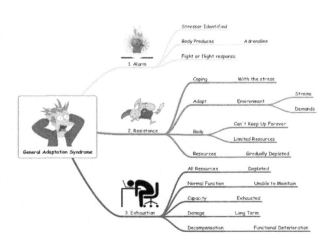

124

14: How the Drama Triangle in Your Dreams Affects Your Health

We know that adrenaline, norepinephrine, and other stress hormones collect in the body when the fight or flight response is activated. In waking life, we can metabolize them by fighting or running. However, when you are anticipating a stress like giving a speech, you can't do either. A similar situation is created very night when you sleep. During your dreams your central nervous system is paralyzed to keep you from acting out your dreams and thereby hurting yourself.

IDL believes that if you want to stay healthy you need to learn to perceive and respond to stressful dreams as wake-up calls. Reenacting the Drama Triangle in one form or another, in dream after dream, can't be good for your health. You might ask, "How can I be stressed if I am unconscious?"

"How can something affect me that I don't even remember?" Here is an analogy. Every time you eat something it affects you for better or for worse. If it's toxic it will harm your body whether or not you are aware of its toxicity. Samples of Beethoven's hair showed that he went deaf and eventually died due to lead poisoning, probably from the pewter mugs he drank from during his life.

Similarly, dreams and nightmares that arouse a fight or flight response in you release powerfully corrosive stress chemicals into your body --whether or not you remember any dreams. When you go to bed worried, your dreams are more likely to be filled with anxiety-causing themes of inadequacy and failure in an attempt to address your fear. If you take as a genuine threat something that is only a dream experience, your body cannot tell the difference. For instance, if you dream of public speaking and being embarrassed and humiliated because the audience is laughing at you and walking out, this is your reality. You will respond as if these events happened to you in real life and your body will go into its normal reactions to stress. This may be one reason why psychotherapy is ineffective with many people. They leave the session feeling good, but at night in their dreams they regress into the Drama Triangle and habitual emotional reactivity and mental delusions, thereby undercutting their progress and increasing the likelihood they will wake up in the morning anxious, depressed, or both.

So how does the Drama Triangle in my dreams undermine my health and peace of mind? Dream threats are typically experienced as real when they are in fact self-created manifestations of the Drama Triangle. While you may dream you are fighting or fleeing, that does nothing to neutralize the powerful hormones that are building up in your tissues as a physiological response to perceived threat. Because they are not dissipated by running or fighting, these hormones act like battery acid, attacking the weakest link in your body's defense system.

Given enough time and enough repeated exposure to these night time assaults on the body, caused by addiction to the Drama Triangle, one person may catch some bug because their immune system is depleted; another person may develop arthritis because their auto-immune system goes haywire. Another person may develop high blood pressure and cardiovascular disease, while yet another may develop insomnia or ulcers. Still others may show no effect whatsoever. While genetic predisposition partially determines which system is most likely to collapse beneath the onslaught of these biochemicals, the depth of your submersion in the Drama Triangle makes an enormous difference in how deep you immerse yourself in physiological toxins, for how long, and how quickly you recover from it.

Fortunately, normal physical activity helps to metabolize and eliminate toxic stress chemicals, which is one reason why regular exercise is so important. If you don't do something physical to metabolize these powerful stress hormones, over time they can destroy your resistance to disease. However, most of us assure ourselves that this is not happening to us. We think about the walking that we do, the exercise that we get, the efforts we make to handle our feelings and responsibilities in ways that don't allow stress hormones to build up in us. Yet we still get sick; our organs break down and we start feeling our age. While some of this is inevitable, how much of it is due to genes and natural processes of aging and how much of it is the result of unnecessary stress due to immersion in the Drama Triangle not only during our waking relationships, but in our thinking and dreams?

How does IDL reduce the Drama Triangle in dreams? IDL short-circuits this process by re-framing your perception of both waking and dreaming sources of anxiety and depression, so that they need not work themselves out in your dreams. For example, Lorna dreamed that she was in her apartment, up to her waist in water. She was not feeling particularly in danger, although she was worried about all the water damage. The water was, in her dream perception, in the role of Persecutor while she was in the role of victim. Dreams like this tend to reinforce life scripts that say, "The world is a dangerous place, full of overwhelming threats, and I am a powerless victim of those threats."

While this dream was somewhat stressful, it is more like a typical dream than a full-blown nightmare. It just as easily could have never been remembered. However, even if it had not been recalled, both the physiological stress processes during the dream and the emotional conclusions that Lorna drew during the dream would have occurred, undercutting both her health and her peace of mind. Lorna's recall of her dream provided her with an opportunity to not only understand the Drama Triangle in the three realms in her life but allowed her to take steps to defuse them to limit future needless physical and psychological damage.

When the Water was interviewed, it said, "I am all the medications that Lorna is taking for her back pain. I am tranquilizing her because she is afraid of feeling how bad the pain may be. She is being swamped by her fear. If she doesn't stop taking us she is not going to get well. Also, by taking us she does not face up to how her fear keeps her trapped in her apartment. She is afraid to go out because then something else bad might happen to her."

This statement by water brings together elements no dream interpreter ever will. You will not read in any guide to dream symbology that water is a symbol for medicine and while it is possible that Lorna would make this association, it is unlikely. How likely is it that any interpreter would associate water not only to medicine but back pain medicine, as well as to fear of pain and how that is associated with her staying trapped in her apartment. Yet in one statement the water makes all of these important and significant connections.

Lorna had been injured in a rear-end collision. Years previously she had sustained a head injury from a freak accident when a falling tree limb hit her. Now, as before, she was afraid to go outside. By listening to the water in her dream Lorna was able to see that her fear was paralyzing her and causing her to take too much pain medication, which was swamping her with sedation. The water was no longer perceived as her Persecutor; instead it took the role of Helper, providing her with important and useful information to understand not only how she was her own worst enemy but pointing her toward what she needed to do to stop creating needless fears.

Armed with this information, Lorna told her doctor that she wanted to cut back on the pain meds. The doctor was upset with her, feeling that she was non-compliant and attempting to doctor herself. The doctor was responding as he had been taught, to her pain symptoms, rather than recognizing how her pain medication itself was a defense against a more fundamental problem – her long-term fear. Her doctor, who probably saw himself as a Helper, was in the Role of Rescuer but in fact in the Role of Persecutor in that he was contributing to Lorna's physiological and psychological dysfunctions. Lorna had to change doctors. When she finally decreased taking the pain meds she immediately became less groggy and less fearful. She could now feel her pain, so she could more accurately tell her new doctor where she hurt so he could help her. Clearly, if Lorna had not listened to a relatively insignificant and typical dream she might have made her recovery longer and much more complicated.

Her dream and what she did with the recommendations that she derived from it is an example of how IDL works to move people out of the Drama Triangle in the three realms of relationships, thought and dreaming.

Arthur Seligman has described something very similar to Selye's *General Adaptation Syndrome* in his explanation of depression as learned helplessness. He explains how cows, when stuck in a bog, will bellow and struggle ferociously to get free. After a while, if their efforts are to no avail, they will struggle less; they have entered the adaptive phase of Selye's General Adaptation Syndrome. If they continue to be sucked down into the bog, they will put up one last heroic struggle before drowning. Seligman noted that cows that are trapped in bogs and yet do not die learn not to struggle; they stop trying to get out, even if they could. This is adaptation to the ongoing stress of Selye's second stage of his General Adaptation Syndrome and resembles our habituation to chronic immersion in the Drama Triangle in our waking relationships, our thoughts and in our dreams.

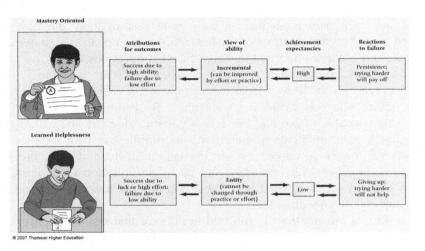

(Picture from Windra.info)

Seligman noted that some of these hopelessly trapped cows that were rescued from bogs by farmers would head right back into the bog again! Do we not do the same when we return to the Drama Triangle and to our addictions? Could it be possible that we do something similar in our dreams? Just as we can get addicted to worry, horror movies or creepy detective thrillers, could it be that we get addicted to creating drama-filled dream vignettes that increase our stress and keep us sick? Repetitive, stressful dreams and nightmares appear to point to such a conclusion.

If we want to protect our health it is not enough to think good thoughts, take our vitamins and be politically correct. We need to eliminate the Drama Triangle in the three realms. We need to learn how to make dreaming as positive an experience as we possibly can. IDL not only teaches us how to recognize and neutralize drama stress; it amplifies forces in consciousness that actively support health, whether awake or asleep.

14: How the Drama Triangle in Your Dreams Affects Your Health

What is the most helpful way to view my dreams to move out of the Drama Triangle? It is wise to treat both your dreams and your life events as wake-up calls. When you interview dream characters, particularly Persecutors, such as monsters, attackers, accidents or natural disasters they will generally say that their purpose is to get your attention, to wake you up. You can test this theory for yourself by doing your own interviews, and you are encouraged to do so. Whether dream and waking events are, in reality, wake-up calls, approaching them as if they are moves us out of the Drama Triangle because we are not perceiving experience in terms of persecution, rescuing or victimization. Instead, both dream and waking experiences are seen as helping when properly listened to in an deep and integral way. Doing so allows you to reframe unpleasant, uncomfortable, painful, confusing or irrelevant dream and life events as teaching experiences that support your further development.

15: Medicine and the Drama Triangle

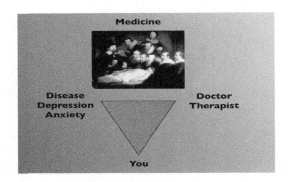

Many people, perhaps most, who go see doctors or mental health professionals, are going to get rescued. They see that professional in the role of the Rescuer and themselves as the Victim of their injury, illness, problem or condition. The doctor will rescue them by giving them a pill or doing surgery, reducing their stress or teaching them life skills. When the doctor succeeds, it reinforces all three roles. The doctor really *is* a rescuer! You, the patient, really were a victim! The condition really was your persecutor! In this way, healing perpetuates the underlying disease: the belief in the reality of the Drama Triangle.

The view of Integral Deep Listening is that your health problems, whatever they may be, are not persecutors at all. They are best approached as if they are wake-up calls. This is a neutral to positive formulation. It keeps you from being in conflict with the part of yourself that the illness represents. Such conflicts add stress and block healing. Viewing your ailments and disabilities as wake-up calls keeps you out of the victim role and from going through life putting health care professionals and their treatments in the role of Rescuer.

15: Medicine and the Drama Triangle

Interviewing Physical Aches, Pains, and Ailments Using IDL

"Eat some grass, and call me in the morning."

   Physical ailments are often experienced as Persecutors within the Drama Triangle. Doing so puts us in a conflictual and powerless relationship with ourselves, forcing us to seek rescuing. In such emotionally-charged contexts we are less likely to make objective, realistic decisions about our health.
   Barb interviewed her chronic back pain which she associated with the color red. A red cloud filling the room condensed into a Black Boulder:
Black Boulder, please tell me what you look like and what you are doing?
I am about three inches round, wedged in Barb's back… like a pain in the ass!
Black Boulder, what do you like most about yourself? What are your strengths?
I get Barb's attention. She pays attention to me!
Black Boulder, what do you dislike most about yourself?
That I hurt people. I don't like to hurt people but it is the only way to wake Barb up. She needs to wake up to some things!
Black Boulder, if you could change Barb's life any way you wanted, would you? How?
I probably would not change it. It is in her best interest.
Black Boulder, what aspect of Barb do you represent or most closely personify?
Her ability to make herself known.

15: Medicine and the Drama Triangle

Black Boulder, if you could live Barb's waking life for her, how would you live it differently?
I would have her eat right, exercise, stop drinking... not stay around Mike so much.
Black Boulder, if you could live Barb's waking life for her today, would you handle her three life issues differently? If so, how?
I would have her lose weight, stop drinking and exercise. She could be a flight attendant again but she may be too old physically. She needs to get her stamina back. It won't be like it was before. She needs to find something where she can lose herself in service to others...maybe the Red Cross. Mike is a very negative influence on her. It is sickening, like her pain. He is making himself sick.
Black Boulder, in what life situations would it be most beneficial for Barb to imagine that she is you and act as you would?
When she needs to be strong and awake to what needs to be changed for her benefit.
Black Boulder, why do you think you are in Barb's life?
To wake her up and get her to move... to focus on what needs to be done.
Black Boulder, how would you score yourself from 0-10 in confidence, empathy, wisdom, acceptance, peace of mind, and witnessing?
confidence 10; empathy 8; wisdom 10; acceptance 10; peace of mind 8; witnessing 9.
Black Boulder, what would it take for Barb to live her life as if she completely manifested these six core characteristics of her authentic self?
She should strike out on her own... take care of her body and soul.
Barb, what have you heard yourself say?
I need to recognize and respect my soul's yearnings. Be true to my soul.
Barb, what have you learned from this experience? How can you use it in your waking life?
To make me wake up and take action.

From the Boulder's perspective its purpose is to wake her up and that until she does so and takes some action, it is actually in Barb's best interest for it to stay! How many people take such an attitude toward their chronic aches and pains?
The Boulder is also saying in effect, "You see me as a Persecutor, but that is not how I see myself. I am trying to get your attention to get you to wake up so that you will stop doing things that create drama and suffering and start doing things that will make your life flow." The Boulder, based on its comments, doesn't see itself in the Drama Triangle, but perhaps it is still in the role of Rescuer. One can always ask a character such a question and see if it gives a reasonable response. It may agree and say, "Yes, I am in the role of Rescuer, and that's the best that can be done in this situation." Or it may say, "No, I am not in the role of Rescuer, because I am not saying I will go away. I will stay until Barb listens to me!"
The Boulder wants Barb to make specific, concrete changes in her health and her relationship with Mike. Are these just Barb's goals or do they represent inner

perspectives she does not own, or are they some combination of both? The high scores that Boulder gives itself in the six core qualities imply that the boulder is a personification of some potential or prospective identity she may or may not grow into.

Clearly, there are many other questions that can be asked the Black Boulder. This example provides a structure to start an ongoing dialoging process. Sometimes IDL serves to heighten awareness of where and how we are stuck in the Drama Triangle; at other times, as when people design and follow an integral life plan based on character recommendations, IDL becomes a pathway out of drama, *dukkha,* and needless suffering. What makes interviewing your dream characters and your life issue personifications a *yoga* is that ongoing process, which is a *disciplined application.*

Hearing inner truth is one thing; using it to motivate you to make changes that are real, lasting, and positive is quite another. Barb had to decide whether to put the recommendations of her Black Boulder to the test by following its advice in her life. That's the only way that she would be able to know for herself whether IDL actually does what it claims to do. Unfortunately, this is not easy for any of us!

There are reasons why you remain comfortably stuck in your maladaptive and dysfunctional patterns, and they aren't going to go away just because some imaginary Black Boulder comes along and says they should. We require a structure and accountability. This is why most people benefit by seeking out an IDL Coach or Practitioner to help them to create and follow an integral life practice for implementing reasonable recommendations that come out of their interviews.

Interviewing a Rash

Carol was worried about a persistent rash that had moved from her legs to her forearms. The rash was a persistent Persecutor and Carol was its Victim. Often all one wants from a dream or an IDL interview is rescuing within the Drama Triangle, and who is to say that is not better in the short run, even if in the long run it reinforces the Drama Triangle itself?

When Carol gave a color to her skin irritation it became blood red, as if it had been exposed to oxygen. The red color filled the room and then condensed into a red plastic ball that was hollow and filled with air. It said, "I am most comfortable being in front of Carol. What I like best about myself is that I am an object of entertainment through her bouncing and kicking me around. I like that I have a tough outer surface. If you bounce me I can bounce back. I'm not fragile. I most closely personify Carol's desire to be mobile and to do more. If I were in charge of Carol's life, I would move around more without worry about having the money to do it. I would find more activities to enjoy. Carol is her own worst enemy when she worries. I don't worry. I'm calm and peaceful. If Carol felt the way, I do all the time she would be at peace. She would be able to live her life to its fullest."

Because Red Ball didn't know anything else about why Carol had the irritation of her skin, we decided to ask it directly. The skin irritation said, "I'm aggravating Carol. I like it! I'm a distraction! She focuses on me. I am strong because I have her full attention. I am powerful! I am in control! I keep Carol from going forward. New pursuits cause me to itch. If Carol moves forward I won't exist! By keeping her miserable, I exist and she stays distracted from her fear of growing and changing. I'm trying to keep her from going forward. I most closely personify Carol's hesitation. I would recommend that Carol find another distraction: moving around and enjoying life. If she moved forward I would go away."

We can see that the Rash is indeed in the role of Persecutor and enjoys it because of the power and control it has. We might call these "secondary gains," but notice they do not accrue to the purported Victim, as most secondary gains do, but to the Persecuting rash. But notice also that the Rash sees itself as a Rescuer.

This interview raises all sorts of fascinating questions. Why would a chronic skin rash express itself as a hollow red ball that sees itself as an object of entertainment that is tough and not fragile? Red Ball says that it is a personification of Carol's desire to move around more and to find more activities that she enjoys. It is calm, peaceful, and doesn't worry, unlike Carol. Therefore, it is not merely a comfortable reflection of Carol's waking perspective. The implication is that Carol can become the red ball when she doesn't want to worry, but what does this have to do with her getting rid of her rash?. There is a further implication that Carol's worry has something to do with her persistent rash. When we interviewed the rash it told us that it works to keep Carol safe by not taking on new activities, the very things that Red Ball is recommending that she do. Skin Irritation said, "These new pursuits cause me to itch. If Carol moves forward I won't exist." The Skin Irritation said that it personified Carol's hesitation about trying new things. We then asked Red Ball what it thought about what Skin Irritation said. At this point Red Ball came up with a clear diagnosis for Carol's rash: "Carol is trying to break out or itching to get away from things in her life. Carol taking action will get rid of the rash. If Carol didn't worry the rash would go away."

Now who is to say that any of this is real or accurate? We are merely collecting other perspectives and then supporting Carol's experiments in living from those that are healthy and that hold promise. The Red Ball sees the rash as a real world, physiological signifier of Carol's issue of, "breaking out and itching

15: Medicine and the Drama Triangle

to get away from things in her life." While this is reminiscent of the types of metaphorical associations to diseases that one finds in the works of Louise Hay, the difference is that these are internally provided rather than externally provided in a "one size fits all" formula that may or may not ring true for you, like symbolic interpretations in dream dictionaries. Red Ball agreed that Carol needed to both take action and work on not worrying. Understanding that her rash might well get worse if she started doing more things, she wanted to see what would happen when she persisted. We developed an integral life practice for Carol that identified specific small ways that she could begin moving forward in her life that were supported by Red Ball and Skin Irritation. They involved walking daily for exercise, looking for another job, and joining a group of people interested in learning to meditate. As she began to do these things the skin irritation first got worse. Then it started going away. After a month both the rash and the skin irritation were gone.

It is not unusual for our pains and physical health problems to state that they exist to protect us from doing things that are outside our comfort zone. When this is fully understood, we stop blaming ourselves for our problems or seeing them as our adversaries. They simply act as defenses that are the same time wake-up calls that these defenses need to be listened to, because they have taken over our lives.

By such a process, perceived Persecutors can become wake-up calls that do not require rescuers or throw us into oppositional, Victim status. IDL does not offer miraculous or immediate cures for life's challenges. Instead, it offers a pathway to authentic healing, balancing and transformation that is a byproduct of listening to and following the recommendations of both wounded and potential perspectives.

Dreams, Cancer and the Drama Triangle

15: Medicine and the Drama Triangle

Margo shared the following dream that illustrates the power and pervasiveness of the Drama Triangle in our dreams. "I am in a room with a bunch of people that I don't know. Everyone there has been diagnosed as having cancer, including a man who is there. A woman that I am talking to had been diagnosed as having cancer in her left hand that had not spread. I tell her that this idea is very archaic, but why don't you just cut your hand off? Then you don't have to die."

It was pretty obvious to Margo, in her dream, as it would be to most observers, that the cancer is a Persecutor. It kills people. When interviewed the cancer confirmed this with remarks such as, "I like a lot that I am inside all these people. That's what I do. That's how I live. I like being in this woman's hand. It won't be long before I'm other places. I love that I'm uncontrollable. I can do anything I want to do. Nobody can stop me. I like the conversation about cutting off her hand. It's amusing. I'll still spread. People should be desperately terrified of me." We can conclude that the cancer is viewed by this dreamer as an abuser and persecutor and plays those roles within the Drama Triangle.

The room, the people, the lady, and the hand all see themselves as victims of the cancer in various ways. For instance, the room said, "I don't like the cancer all these people have. That's the reason all this negative energy is inside me. I dislike myself. I feel like I'm full of a bunch of negative energy." The room feels overwhelmed by something negative that is greater than itself. It feels powerless to do anything about it. The consequence for the room, as is often the case for us, is that we end up not liking ourselves because we feel weak and out of control. The room personifies Margo in the role of Victim in the Drama Triangle.

The dreamer sees herself as a Rescuer. She says, "I love myself. I hate the diagnosis of cancer because it's a bad thing to have cancer. I hate that everybody has cancer because it's bad because it will kill them. I believe that all these people are going to die if they have cancer."

"I like the idea of cutting off this woman's hand because it is a solution to stopping the cancer." Rescuers generally have high opinions of themselves because they see themselves as providing the necessary solution. Rescuers are also sure they understand both the problem and what needs to be done to fix it, just as this dreamer does. Since all of these characters are aspects of the dreamer, she is Persecutor, Victim, and Rescuer to herself all at the same time. The larger question is then raised, is there a solution to this persecution by the cancer within the context of the Drama Triangle? If all the characters are within that perceptual cognitive distortion, playing by the same rules, within the Drama Triangle, where is the objectivity going to come from necessary to move to some sort of integration? The answer is, "It's not." If there are no voices, either in a dream or in a waking context that express perspectives outside the Drama Triangle then there is only one possibility: to embrace a turn of the wheel of karma, for the characters at the Mad Hatter's Tea Party to change seats, remaining at the table, in a context of derangement.

Margo's dream demonstrates the inevitability of assuming the burden of all three roles when we take on any of them, although we do not realize it at the time. It also demonstrates that *you cannot abuse another person without abusing that part of yourself that they personify.* You cannot rescue another person without disempowering the parts of yourself that they personify. You cannot victimize another person without creating war within yourself. To the extent that others, whether in waking life, dreams or some other state of consciousness personify aspects of ourselves, how we treat them is how we are treating those aspects of ourselves which they represent.

Might there be a healthier perspective from which to approach our fears, one that does not cultivate the Drama Triangle or reinforce a mindset of victimization by forces in life we can't control? By practicing IDL in response to her dreams about cancer, Margo could reduce the repeated mental and physiological stressors of experiencing herself persecuted, victimized, and avoiding the real issues through self-rescuing behaviors. Both her dreams and her work with them could begin to function as a form of preventive health care. She can learn to listen to wake-up calls internally, in her dreams, before they can externalize as crises in relationships, waking events, and her physical health.

In contrast to Margo's own anxiety in her dream, as well as the perspectives of persecution and victimization expressed by the cancer and other people in the room that had cancer, her interview with the woman in the dream who had cancer in her hand was surprising. She said, "I don't think the cancer is going to do anything to me. I'm not going to cut my hand off. I don't believe this is going to be necessary because it is not going to spread."

This is not the comment of a Victim, which the dreamer assumed the lady to be.

We can see that the very assumption that victimization is happening tends to create a Rescuer response within us, as it did within Margo.

Consequently, part of the process of outgrowing the Drama Triangle is to move beyond assumptions of victimization, whether regarding others or ourselves.

But was this wishful thinking? Would following this advice be a foolish avoidance of a real problem, the spread of a lethal cancer? How could Margo tell?

Margo also interviewed this woman's hand. It said, "I know she won't cut me off. I'm a part of her and she will be able to get rid of the cancer. What I like best about being in this dream is that I am connected to this woman and she'll take care of me." This hand does not see itself as a Victim either. It has confidence that its needs will be fulfilled. This is a trusting part of Margo, one that was not obvious from the dream narrative.

Just because we react to some circumstance we often assume that this is the best or most appropriate way of looking at the situation and responding to it, just as Margo did in the dream by believing her recommendation of amputation was appropriate.

Decisions based on reactivity are rarely well-thought out and satisfactory in the long run. IDL demonstrates that there always exist authentic perspectives we can access that witness our fear with greater empathy, wisdom, and peace than we ourselves do. Once you take the time to look at your life from the perspective of non-reactive parts of yourself, as Margo did when she became the woman and her hand, empathetic detachment is experienced. This is different from an intellectual gloss on pain. Such experiences can change your perception of your fear, your disease, and your life choices fundamentally. Reactivity loses its reality, necessity, and inevitability. You create space for yourself to breathe and to live well within almost any condition. You still are responsible for making the best choice you can, and it may not give you the results you want, even in a life and death situation like Margo's. Rather than providing certainty, IDL provides a deeper degree of comfort with whatever is decided and with its outcome.

The benefit of interviewing a variety of dream characters is that you are provided with a number of perspectives on problems about which you must make decisions. As a result, you are more likely to make decisions that are consensus – representing a greater good for a greater percentage of those perspectives invested in growing your life. To this end, Margo also interviewed the cancer. It said, "My strengths are that I can do anything. Nobody can stop me. I'm very strong, very confident. If I were in charge of Margo's waking life she would be like me. She would have confidence and just do it. It would be helpful for Margo to imagine that she is me when she is overwhelmed or things are a little bit scary. She just needs to be confident." By becoming the cancer Margo was accepting the abuser within herself.

This allowed her to see and accept the strengths that are inherent in those parts of life that scared her. The point of view of cancer allowed Margo to experientially reframe her deepest fears as resources and inner strengths that she had disowned.

She could own the confidence of Cancer.

IDL allowed Margo to undo her dream reinforcement of her fears of getting sick and dying. Without the practice of IDL Margo would have continued to send powerful visual and emotional affirmations to her body that she was sick, that she had reason to be afraid, and that she was a helpless Victim. Margo began to see that while this dream seemed to be about victimization and abuse, it not only did not have to be seen that way, it *wasn't* that way.

Margo's experience is the norm for people who practice IDL. The more that you deeply listen to emerging potentials the less inclination you will have to feed scarcity, separation, or ignorance within yourself. You will find yourself outgrowing many of the stuck places in your life. Notice, however, that Margo is

15: Medicine and the Drama Triangle

still going to get sick and die at some point. Life is much more concerned with *how* you live the life you have than that you live forever. Margo's interview, just like IDL, are not about eliminating stress, disease, or death, but about outgrowing the factors that destroy the quality of life that you are living, and increasing your ability to be fully alive.

IDL will teach you not to take yourself and the absurdities of the human predicament so seriously. We walk onto the stage of life, play our parts, take our bows, and are gone, melting into all players, all audiences, and all producers.
IDL can demonstrate to you that the enlightened states of awareness that you seek coexist with your everyday awareness right now. They are immediately accessible, all the time, if you only know where to look to find them and learn to recognize them. Because these states regularly crop up personified as dream characters and personifications of your life issues that are interviewed by IDL, you are regularly provided with personalized metaphors for advanced states of consciousness. These are not merely visual metaphors; they are experiential openings involving a profound shift in awareness into spaces of vast equanimity, inspiring fearlessness, deep empathy, piercing wisdom, and profound acceptance.

16: The Wizard of Oz and the Merging of Waking and Night Time Dreams in the Drama Triangle

The Wizard of Oz, perhaps the most beloved American movie, contains terrific examples of the Drama Triangle. Dorothy gains our sympathy by playing such a wonderful Victim. First, she gets uprooted from her Kansas home by a nasty persecuting tornado. Then she has a highly vengeful witch out to get her. Monkeys come and capture her. She is victimized by the Great and Powerful Oz who she sees first as a Rescuer and then as a Persecutor. But like Dorothy, the Wizard is a poor, helpless Victim, who was blown to Oz in his hot air balloon, and just wants to go home.

Dorothy is also a wonderful little Rescuer. She rescues the Tin Woodman from rust and the Scarecrow from his pole after accidentally rescuing the Munchkins from the Wicked Witch of the East by crushing her with a falling house. She even rescues Oz from the hypocrisy of his charade. What aspects of herself is Dorothy rescuing?

Because Dorothy chooses to play the Rescuer and the Victim, she also ends up playing the Persecutor. She gets to smack the Cowardly Lion on the nose, call Oz names, and murder the Wicked Witch of the West. While Dorothy naturally sees the death of the Wicked Witch of the East as an accident, it occurs in her dream, which means that she is the persecuting house as well as the victimized Wicked Witch of the East. Just who and what is Dorothy killing out of her awareness?

And what about that Wicked Witch? Apparently Frank Braun, the creator of *The Wizard of Oz,* did not even give her a proper name, so as to suitably demonize

16: The Wizard of Oz and the Merging of Waking and Night Time Dreams in the Drama Triangle

her. Was she not attempting to bring justice to the person who killed her sister who she saw as a helpless victim? Might Dorothy be found guilty of two counts of negligent homicide for her part in the killing of two people?

Part of the importance and power of *The Wizard of Oz* is that it draws no clear distinction between the Drama Triangle in waking life and dreams. When we are dreaming, we think we are awake, just as Dorothy does. We respond in dreams as if we were dealing with real life situations and threats.

In the *Wizard of Oz* Dorothy is dreaming, victimized by her ignorance of her own ability to take herself home at any moment. At any time she can choose to step out of the Drama Triangle of her own personal dream and wake up. The witch and wizard are not her enemies, as they are personifications of aspects of herself. Her lack of lucidity and objectivity, as well as her inability to access a context that includes but transcends the Drama Triangle, is her enemy.

Simply realizing that she is dreaming, that is, becoming lucid in the dream, does not imply Dorothy moves out of drama. She could conceivably wake up in the dream and kill the witch and wizard or transform Oz into paradise or simply do what most of us do – wake up, which is to become relatively lucid. We then think, "That was just a dream!" but without understanding or changing any of the conditions that created it in the first place. Therefore, it is important to understand that lucidity, in and of itself, is not a solution to the Drama Triangle. It is not enough to recognize you are in delusion. You have to have the wisdom to respond to delusion outside the Drama Triangle. This is something that you can and should do whether you are lucid in a dream or not.

For example, Margo could, without realizing she is dreaming, recognize that she is in the Drama Triangle in relation to the cancer and the other characters in the dream. She could then ask herself, "What could I do now, in this dream, that would respond to this situation in a way that would keep me out of the Drama Triangle?" There is no one right answer; it changes with the individual and the circumstances. However, this sort of question is an example of a much healthier response to the Drama Triangle, whether we are asleep and dreaming or awake. It can lead us to do simple things like ask questions to get more information. In terms of Transactional Analysis, this would be to stay in the informational Adult ego state instead of jumping into an emotionally reactive Child ego state or a confrontational or rescuing Parental ego state.

At the end of the *Wizard of Oz* Dorothy wakes up, realizes he was dreaming, but largely misses the import of what she was experiencing. Much like near death experiences, Dorothy returns to waking life with an overflowing sense of gratitude and a new appreciation for what she has previously taken for granted. The problem is that like Dorothy, we will tend to fall back asleep again into our daily routines and expectations that tomorrow will be more or less like today. IDL

16: The Wizard of Oz and the Merging of Waking and Night Time Dreams in the Drama Triangle

interviewing helps us to remember and internalize the endless creativity that is always available as a preventive against falling deeply asleep within the Drama Triangle.

17: Healing Social Nightmares

"Most Americans have no idea that what we are fed by the news media is nothing more than a portrayal of what powerful corporations want us to believe, that what happens to pass as education is as often as not mere propaganda, that what we learn in church may have very little or nothing to do with the truth, that what our parents teach us may be nothing more than an accumulation of their own personal biases, no doubt a rather subtle modification of what they were taught by their parents. And through such a process, governments and nations around the world wield control as to what their citizens, believe, value, and do."

Doug Soderstrom

Social nightmares are collective externalizations of the Drama Triangle into our waking culture and shared social spaces. When you learn to recognize the Drama Triangle you can look out at the world and see it all around you. What to do? We cannot wait for government to show leadership on this issue. In fact, it has done the exact opposite. Instead of waking up, government in the early 2000's fell more deeply into a Drama Triangle by blaming others (terrorists and Russians). It used this as justification to avoid responsibility, extend its control worldwide and destroy citizen rights to privacy.

Just as you learned to recognize the Drama Triangle in your relationship by first recognizing how it exists in the three realms in your own life, so your perception of the world will change as you yourself outgrow your addiction to the Drama Triangle. As you learn to see events in the three realms as wake-up calls you move your perception of society and governance from the three roles to the much more neutral recognition that all political and social events, good, bad and ugly, are best approached as if they are wake-up calls. The question for you then becomes, "Am I listening?"

You cannot wait for your government, media and educators to evolve out of the Drama Triangle. You have to decide when and if you are sick of your multiple addictions to the drama imbedded in your macrocosm and then decide what to do about it. You can then choose to stop putting yourself into an adversarial relationship with the parts of yourself that the Drama Triangle represents, but instead to practice deep listening in an integral sort of way. You can accept responsibility to practice IDL for yourself, in your own personal and business relationships.

There is something to learn about ourselves in everyone and everything, particularly in those people and events that upset us the most. Current events are as much about the Drama Triangle and as addictive as anything else. If you find yourself habitually invested with world events or becoming emotionally involved with them, why not do some interviews around them? You can do single character interviews around political and world figures that evoke strong emotions in you or you can do complicated, sophisticated multiple character interviews using .Dream Sociometry, which demonstrate the roles of Persecutor, Victim and Rescuer embedded in every social and political nightmare, crisis and dilemma. You can also interview your feelings around some current event. For example, if you are enraged by what some politician has done, why not let your rage turn into some animal or object and interview it?

Through deep listening you will reframe current events in a way that includes but transcends the Drama Triangle. You will learn to take responsibility for your response to world events, good, bad, and ugly. At the same time you will learn to not take responsibility for that which is not about you. You will first grow out of personalization, which is an emotional cognitive distortion, and then into cosmic humor, or the ability to smile at your tendency to become entangled in drama. The more that you take responsibility for your relationships and your planet, while refusing to take responsibility for someone else's mess, the more effective will be your efforts to awaken within your life dream. Your ability to empathize with other perspectives that create your reality will increase. Your willingness to focus locally, in your own community, to make improvements in quality, quantity and sustainability of collective daily life will lift you up as you raise others. It's time. The world needs you.

*18: How Our World Views Keep Us Stuck
in the Drama Triangle*

18: The Drama Triangle and Economic Sanity

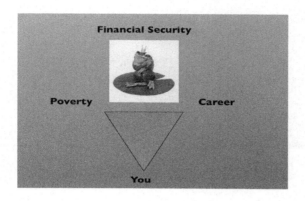

Money is the ugly toad that, if you can only catch and kiss, will turn into the handsome prince of security, status and freedom. You may think it is the root of all evil, but you want it and need it. You look for various ways to be rescued by money. You get a job. When you find it doesn't get you off the treadmill, you study hard and start a career. The income you earn compels you to stay in work that is not what you thought it would be. Now, you can't start over because you're trapped: you have to keep working to pay your bills. Perhaps you get "lucky" and find financial security. Money *has* rescued you from poverty! You are now secure and have status and freedom, right? The Drama Triangle has validated itself.

If you interview most wealthy people, they will tell you that they don't have security, status or freedom, compared to some bigger toad sitting on some bigger lily pad. If you spend your life trying to catch and kiss ugly toads, don't be too surprised if you mostly end up sweaty, dirty and, perhaps, covered with warts.

How in your life have you viewed money and financial security as a rescuer? How has that worked out for you? What could you do instead? Is it possible to have a healthier attitude toward money and financial security? If so, what would that be?

18: How Our World Views Keep Us Stuck in the Drama Triangle

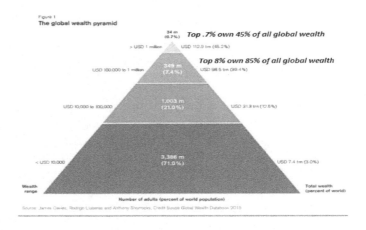

Figure 1
The global wealth pyramid

Source: James Davies, Rodrigo Lluberas and Anthony Shorrocks, Credit Suisse Global Wealth Databook 2015

There never has been and never will be an economic system that is fair; the more its participants operate within the Drama Triangle the more unfair it becomes. When people maximize their own profit at the expense of others they are Persecutors. Adam Smith's "invisible hand" assumes there are no losers in a predatory, abusive system which maximizes benefits for oneself. In truth, under such a system everyone loses, because everyone is exploited. As Plato pointed out, "Honesty is for the most part less profitable than dishonesty." Even the few "winners" live in a valueless, hollowed-out culture which sanctions the plundering of resources and ecosystems until they go extinct. Jared Diamond in *Collapse* demonstrates this principle as a human economic inevitability – unless the economic, cultural, social and behavioral rules are radically changed. Capitalism, and economics in general, is the fine art of financially taking advantage of others and getting them to like it. It is about short-term gain while ignoring long-term consequences unless one is first educated as to those consequences and then incentives are put into place that reward all players for playing by the same set of rules, as in fishery regulations to bring back over-fished areas or to keep stocks from being depleted. Much of this unfair system is maintained by preying on the ignorance of consumers. For example, both "trickle down" and "austerity" economics demonstrate a hypocritical, dishonest "socialism for the rich, capitalism for the poor." Unfair systems are also maintained by inviting potential opponents in for a portion of the spoils. Socio-cultural conditioning follows the finely-honed principles of propaganda, more courteously called "marketing." History will look back in amazement that the population of the West put up with the siphoning off of so much of its wealth for so long into military expenditures at the cost of basic social stability.

Rather than exploring the infinite variety of ways that people conduct daily

18: How Our World Views Keep Us Stuck in the Drama Triangle

economic transactions within the Drama Triangle, a solution-focus explores the questions, "Are there alternatives to economics within the Drama Triangle? If so, what might they look like?"

Frederic Laloux, in *Reinventing Organizations*, identifies multiple factors that generate economic systems that operate more or less within the Drama Triangle. In those systems that are least enmeshed, collective wealth is distributed from the bottom up, in the form of the distribution of power and decision-making. The societal analogy is to invest wealth in the weakest, the youngest, the least advantaged, the sickest and the oldest. These people then provide resources and positive inputs to society, particularly qualitative benefits by enriching the quality of human interaction. There are quantitative benefits as well, most of which cannot be anticipated. As the sense of security of a society shifts from external defense to maximization of the talents of its citizens, creativity and productivity are encouraged. People who are thankful naturally wish to express their gratitude; many will do so in ways that increase the wealth of society.

For those who say that a country or nation-state doesn't have the funds to do this, the appropriate counter-argument is to point out that it doesn't have any better use of tax dollars than to improve the quality of life for its citizens. It can also be pointed out that all other approaches have been tried, such as first feeding the plutocrats or first feeding the military; such approaches have been shown to eventually create massive social unrest. When states divert resources to the bottom of the pyramid the entire pyramid thrives; when it does not, the pyramid sooner or later self-destructs.

http://www.oftwominds.com/blogjan17/labor-economy1-17.html

19: Terrorism and the Drama Triangle

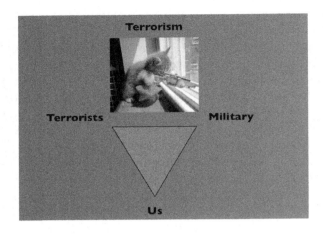

While we can agree that terrorism is a terribly violent act of aggression, we can't seem to agree on is just who the terrorists are. For Israelis, Palestinians are terrorists. For Palestinians, Israelis are terrorists. For the US, Islamic fundamentalists are terrorists; for Islamic fundamentalists, the US government is the terrorist. Who is the Terrorist and who is the Rescuer? The basic problem is that whoever buys into this model has already put themselves into the role of Victim in the Drama Triangle. You can never eliminate terrorism as an individual, society or world community as long as you are in the Drama Triangle.

In the first decades of the 21st century it became obvious that terrorism was created by the West as a way to maintain the financial, power and status benefits for a few that come with maintaining a war economy. Because these ends are highly addictive and self-perpetuating they do not easily yield to moral or rational persuasion. The only ways to stop the game is to change its financial rules, that is, to make war less profitable while no longer allowing yourself to react in fear to fake, manufactured or minimal threats.

IDL addresses terrorism by both clarifying the role of the Persecutor and taking responsibility for it. In fact, the habitual interviewing of emerging potentials makes it highly unlikely that individuals will support institutionalized abuse, which at its worst is state-supported terrorism. This is because one cannot do IDL interviewing without taking responsibility for one's own fear and reactivity. Once fear is no longer displaced onto others it becomes much more likely that solutions to genuine disagreements can be found.

We terrorize ourselves first by projecting our fear onto others and then by assuming that the fears we own, such as self-created dream monsters, represent real fears. Both of these fears are dispelled quickly and thoroughly with IDL interviewing. With only a few such interviews we quickly come to recognize that the circumstances that call for a genuine fear response are few and far between.

20: Global Warming and the Drama Triangle

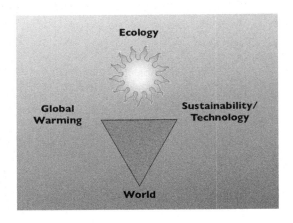

Anything that can cause mass extinctions and destroy all the cities on seacoasts of the world is a Persecutor, right? We need green technologies, educated entrepreneurs, a new world of green workers and supportive government policies to rescue us, right? From the perspective of Big Oil and the majority of the Republican Party in the United States as of 2012, the answer is no. From the perspective of most corporately-owned media, the answer is also no. From these vantage points, global warming is a lie perpetrated on the public by devious progressives, and it is the job of deniers to rescue us and the world from such mythical constructions and wastes of money.

When you look at global warming as a wake-up call, the question is not, "How disruptive does climate have to be before *others* (politicians, corporations, investors) wake up?" Instead, it becomes, "How loud does the wake-up call have to be before *I* hear it and wake up?"

Looking at global warming from within the Drama Triangle invites dramatic decisions that will cause you to end up in the role of the Persecutor in the eyes of others when you change your buying habits (or, on a national level, allocate funds) in ways that disadvantage individual group. It is important to remember that you can never control whether or not others see you in the Drama Triangle, or what role they put you in, or how they will react when you stop playing. All you can do is work hard at identifying it in your life and staying out of it yourself. Beyond that you can educate others and dedicate yourself to making the world a better place. What you can control is whether you fall into the Drama Triangle or not, and when you do, how long you stay in it before you wake up and get out.

Personal and social solutions to global warming that are balanced and lasting

20: Global Warming and the Drama Triangle

require outstanding judgment and dedicated, persistent action. None of that is possible from within the Drama Triangle. Instead, what is generated is more drama at a time when time is precious, and when you need to be clear and out of your own way. While IDL will not solve global warming, it can help you get out and stay out of the Drama Triangle.

Creative people are generating a myriad individual pieces of the solution to global warming. While some of these are being enacted on the level of the UN and individual nation states, most of it is being driven by mayors, entrepreneurs, and individuals. These are occurring in all four quadrants of the human holon, meaning that we are witnessing powerful transformations in behavior, technology, values and interior consciousness. Examples of behavior changes include buying organic, locally and from "fair trade" sources, recycling, energy-saving, using power-saving light bulbs and using energy-saving transportation. Examples of technological responses to global warming include perma, hydro and aquacultures, solar and wind power generation, biomass, whole systems housing and industry solutions, electric batteries and vehicles. Examples of transformation from the realm of values include the sustainability ideas and solutions offered by Jeremy Rifkin, conservation, a deeper understanding of evolutionary ecology, as in trophic cascades, and the Gaia model of James Lovelock. Examples from the realm of interior consciousness include an evolutionary broadening of our individual definition of ourselves to include other races, nations and species. Rather than looking for one of these four areas to "save the day" it is important to recognize that all four of these not only co-create change but, if one is neglected, it acts as a "lagging line" and a break on the others.

While interviewed emerging potentials emphasize the interior collective and individual domains of value and consciousness, dreaming offers extraordinary opportunities for individual creativity and inventiveness while the perspectives of interviewed emerging potentials often offer both examples of healthy interaction and relationship and practical solutions for improving them.

21: Meditation and the Drama Triangle

While Buddha provides a powerful reminder of the relationship between meditation and enlightenment, that he meditates both on and is protected by a seven-headed serpent is a reminder of how meditation tames the mind, emotions and our enchantment by the delusions they create. Integral Deep Listening (IDL) expands on an important and powerful concept from Transactional Analysis, called "the Drama Triangle." Referring to the interactions of the three roles of Persecutor, Victim, and Rescuer in interpersonal relationships, IDL expands the concept by applying the Drama Triangle to two other dimensions of human experience, cognition (thoughts, feelings, images, sensations and our sense of self), and night-time dreams. In addition it calls attention to the relevance of the Drama Triangle for the understanding of mystical and near death experiences.

IDL teaches that it is not enough to identify and avoid the Drama Triangle in your relationships; you need to be able to identify it and avoid it in your thoughts and dreams as well, because these are sources that not only generate drama in your relationships; they make peace of mind impossible. For example, a night spent in anxiety-provoking dreams will create an undercurrent of tension that can start your day off on the wrong foot without you ever remembering a single dream. Meditation is a powerful tool for eliminating the Drama Triangle, primarily in the second of those three dimensions, in your thoughts, feelings, images, and sensations.

IDL understands the Drama Triangle as a modern and psychological reframing of the ancient and classical sources of human misery: *avidya*, or ignorance, *maya*, or illusion, *karma*, or self-generated captivity, *dukkha*, or suffering, and *sin*, or

21: Meditation and the Drama Triangle

separation from God. Most of what people call meditation is unfortunately, in fact cognitive immersion in the Drama Triangle. This is one way of understanding why meditation is aversive, frustrating and unproductive for many people.

The role of *Persecutor* can be understood as abuse of others or self, whether awake or in a dream. Persecutors never consider themselves to be in that role. Instead, they are "defending" or "teaching." Therefore, persecution is determined by the victim of the abuse, not by the abuser, whose judgment is not to be trusted as being empathetic with the perspective of the Victim. Persecutors feel justified and self-righteous; when you have such feelings or argue with someone, or feel a need to "explain" yourself to others, know that you are most likely putting yourself in the role of Persecutor. When you criticize yourself for not meditating correctly or enough you are in the role of Persecutor in relationship to your practice of meditation.

The role of Victim is not victimization, the very real abuse that happens when a child is molested or your car is rear-ended. Instead, the role of Victim is associated with feelings of hopelessness, helplessness, and powerlessness, and "justified" avoidance of responsibility. To a much greater degree than with victimization, Victims choose these feelings and rationalizations. The position of Victim is very powerful because when you are in it you are blameless. "What can anyone expect of me? I'm a victim!" You put yourself in the role of Victim in your meditation when you view yourself battling, sin, impurity, attachment, ignorance, confusion or evil or when you feel powerless against the onslaught of your own feelings, thoughts, images and sensations.

The role of Rescuer is different from a "helper." While a Rescuer jumps in, without waiting for a request, a Helper either waits for a request or asks if help is needed. While a Rescuer just keeps on keeping on, out of a certainty of their good intentions, a Helper checks to see if the help they are giving is indeed useful. While a Rescuer doesn't stop when the job is done but instead takes up another task, out of the goodness of their heart and their confidence in their own motives, a Helper stops and waits for another request. Rescuers think they are altruistic, compassionate and generous when they are actually attempting to validate their own self-worth by demonstrating that they are beyond reproach. A sure tip-off that you are in the rescuer role is how you feel when your desire to "help" is rejected. Rescuers generally feel rejected and unappreciated. They take a refusal to accept their assistance or advice personally. Another sign of rescuing is burn-out from giving more than you get back from life. In meditation, assume that most of the strategies you use to meditate are at foundation types of self-rescuing. The objective, as we shall see, is to find healthier and more productive forms of self-rescuing in meditation that encourage evolution into the position of Helper.

Each of these roles generate the other two. Persecutors become Victims and often conclude that because they are Victims, persecution is justified. When you are self-critical regarding your meditation you put yourself in both Persecutor and Victim roles. Victims persecute both themselves and those around them through their passivity, avoidance and excuse-making. Rescuers are resented because they are basically selfish and manipulative; consequently they are sooner or later seen as the Persecutors they are. For example, in meditation whatever tool that you are taught or use to quiet your mind and center your awareness will tend, at some point, to become a rigid structure that blocks both meditative flow and your own development.

It is relatively easy to identify these three roles in relationships, and indeed, that is where IDL recommends that you start. The next step is to look for ways that you play these three roles in your thoughts. Are you not in the role of Persecutor whenever you criticize yourself? Are you not in the role of Victim whenever you feel helpless, powerless, and out of control? Are you not in the role of Rescuer whenever you indulge in any addiction or avoidance strategy, whether it is eating something that isn't on your diet or surf the internet instead of doing what is on your "to do" list?

The realistic but very uncomfortable assumption to make is that you are in the Drama Triangle all the time, and that life outside of it is a foreign, unfamiliar, and uncomfortable concept and state. While you say you want inner peace, is it not true that when you attempt to find it in meditation you largely end up in the Drama Triangle instead?

You probably meditate to find equanimity, as well as centeredness, balance, clarity, and mindfulness. However, isn't most of the time you spend doing whatever you call meditation filled with both thoughts and feelings, on the one hand, and your attempts to escape from them, on the other? Is this not the Drama Triangle? Let's look more closely at how this works.

Because most people do not know the distinction between rescuing and helping, they view meditation as a form of self-help when they are actually performing acts of self-rescue. To the extent that you meditate to escape from something, such as your thoughts, the stresses of life, or the existential predicament of existence in the world, meditation is an act of self-rescue, is it not? Meditation then becomes a form of escape and avoidance. Hinduism and Buddhism are quite explicit about this. Meditation is for Hinduism an escape from *samsara* into *moksha* and *samadhi*. For Buddhism, meditation is an escape from *avidya*, ignorance, into *nirvana*. For Hinduism, Buddhism and Christianity meditation is an aesthetic escape into rescuing purification. Such formulations put your thoughts and feelings, the world, and life itself, in the role of Persecutor, meaning that meditation can become a conflictual relationship within the Drama Triangle. To the extent that you become addicted to some meditative approach or tool you risk it turning into a Persecutor, even if it is a positive addiction. This is not an argument to not use tools when you meditate but instead a recommendation to

21: Meditation and the Drama Triangle

recognize that like ladders, when they take you to their termination you leave the ladder and proceed on. In many ways, instead of moving you out of the Drama Triangle, meditation can actually reinforce it.

When meditation is assumed to be a form of self-rescue, as it is in both Hinduism and Buddhism, it merely generates more *karma* and suffering through a flight from ignorance and suffering to freedom or *nirvana*. A similar form of self-deception occurs within Christianity. When prayer and meditation are undertaken to become one with God, as it is in Christian mysticism of Theresa of Avila, St. John of the Cross or Meister Eckhart, the implication is that you are not normally one with God. Therefore, prayer and meditation become forms of self-rescue from normalcy, a life of secular separation from God or sin, that actually both affirms and reaffirms the reality of your separation from God.

How do the three ways that a Rescuer is different from a helper show up in meditation? How do you, when you meditate, jump in, without waiting for a request for help? This occurs whenever you react to a thought, feeling, or sensation. Perhaps you feel a pain in your knee. It is one thing to change position to alleviate you pain or even to stop meditating, take care of your knee, and then return to meditation. It is quite another to experience the pain in your knee as a distraction, interruption, or enemy of your attempt to meditate. By doing so you put yourself into conflict with your pain and with yourself. You experience your pain in the role of Persecutor and you are therefore the Victim of it. Now you need to do something to rescue yourself from your pain.

The same holds true of distracting thoughts, unwanted feelings, and pictures that keep floating through your mind. If you are a follower of the traditional yoga of Patanjali or a Zen Buddhist, you repress these things as persecuting distractions within the Drama Triangle, thereby risking giving them both reality and power. If you do mantra meditation, such as Transcendental Meditation, Tibetan Buddhist mantric meditation or Nichiren or Shingon Japanese Buddhist meditation, you practice avoidance via substitution. Your answer to everything that comes up is substitution: you return to repeating your mantra or working your japa mala or rosary.

The problem with practicing meditation within the context of self-rescue is that you turn your mind into a Persecutor and yourself into a Victim. There is no escape, because your practice occurs within the perceptual cognitive distortion called the Drama Triangle. The context of your entire practice can become self-defeating if you do not find ways to compensate for these **insidious** natural tendencies.

IDL proposes an approach to meditation that is designed to recognize the challenges of the Drama Triangle, take them into account, and minimize them. It involves three tools. The first involves applying the distinction between helping and rescuing to your meditations by learning to be vigilant for indicators of the presence of the Drama Triangle, how you meditate within it and the cultivation of a desire to get out of it. Without these self-awarenesses the other two tools will be practiced within the context of the Drama Triangle. The second tool is naming and the third is observation of your breathing.

The question then becomes, "How can I spend most of my time while meditating in the role of Helper?" If a Rescuer jumps in, without waiting for a request, the analogy in meditation is to react to stimuli, whether a pain, sensation, sound, image, thought or feeling instead of simply observing it. Once you understand the distinction between being a self-rescuer and a Helper when you meditate you can then decide what a respectful response will be. Most of the time it will be to simply name or note your thought, feeling, sensation or image and allow your awareness to move into clarity or to name the next stimuli. However, there will be times when a stimuli is persistent and you need to make a plan to deal with it: "I'll call after meditation;" "When I'm done I will note that appointment in my calendar." There will be other times when the stimuli will cause you to want to end your meditation. When that occurs IDL recommends that you once again return to a mental space of relative clarity before stopping in order to put a positive closure on your meditation.

While a Rescuer just keeps on keeping on, out of a certainty of their good intentions, a Helper checks to see if the help they are giving is indeed useful. The best way to do this in the context of meditation is to see if naming, maintaining objectivity and observation of your breath allow you to return to clarity or not. It is also recommended that you interview emerging potentials of your choice after your meditation from time to time to see if the approach you are using is indeed useful at moving you out of the Drama Triangle and into greater alignment with the priorities of your life compass.

A third condition that differentiates Rescuers from Helpers is that Rescuers don't stop when the job is done but instead take up another task, while Helpers stop and wait for another request. The analogy in meditation is to beware of attempts to self-rescue during meditation. One example is to impulsively follow some thought, feeling, sensation or image, forgetting for the moment your intention, why you are meditating. Assume anything that you do or think in mediation is an attempt at self-rescue and observe it rather than mindlessly listening to or following it. If meditation feels like a struggle or you find yourself "burning out" and losing interest in meditating, you have probably been self-rescuing. Your expectations are probably unrealistic and you are trying too hard. You want to partner with your body, mind and emotions when you meditate, not conquer or control them.

There are a number of ways to use your breathing to move you out of the Drama Triangle and keep you there when you meditate. The first and simplest is to use your exhalations to let go of all need to self-rescue, whether by thinking thoughts,

21: Meditation and the Drama Triangle

feeling certain feelings, maintaining a particular posture, meditating for a certain period of time or attaining a certain space of equanimity or inner peace. Counting while you exhale and attempting to make each successive exhalation a bit deeper and longer than the last for a series of three to five breaths are two strategies to keep your attention focused on your exhalations.

Use your exhalations to let go of your need to either avoid or substitute anything for your pain, thoughts, feelings, or images. Stop seeing whatever comes up as something that you need to do anything about or as a request for help. Why? Because although it is easy and simple to interpret any pain, thought, feeling, or image as a request for help, this interpretation lands you in the role of Rescuer within the Drama Triangle. Instead, move to a space of balanced neutrality and non-reactivity. *Then* make a decision about what to do. You may want to intervene in some way or you may not, but the key is to learn to make decisions outside the Drama Triangle, and you cannot and will not if you are reactive or are not in a space of acceptance and inner equanimity.

As a general rule, use meditation as a time and place to cultivate that balanced neutrality and non-reactivity; save problem-solving for later. If you need or want to problem solve, stop meditating, change location and focus on your problem. Then, when you are done, return to your meditation. This teaches several lessons, including flexibility and the priority of meditation.

Of course, using your exhalations in such a way can also become a form of self-rescue; the goal is not to avoid the Drama Triangle all together but to discover tools that move you into increasingly subtle forms of self-rescue, persecution and victimization. This is a much more realistic goal as it is attainable, whereas "enlightenment," "oneness with God," "nirvana," "salvation," the "burning up of all karmas," freedom and perfection are not.

You may recall that the second way that a Rescuer differs from a Helper is in not checking to see if the help that is given really is helpful. Rescuers just "know" that what they are doing is helpful and useful because their intention is so *pure*. How is this different from a parent spanking a child for their own good? How is this different from a parent justifying their abuse by saying, "This hurts me worse than it does you?" How is this different from an individual or country going to war for God, peace or democracy?

IDL deals with this predicament in meditation in several ways. As we have seen, the first is to assume that any intervention you make to deal with a "distraction" in meditation is a form of self-rescuing. If you don't like a thought, feeling, image, or sensation and react to it, assume that you are in the role of Rescuer. Secondly, if it persists, table it and return to meditation, telling yourself that the purpose of meditation is not to address everything that comes up but rather to amplify balance, centeredness, clarity, and inner peace. Be structured but not rigid, like a nurturing parent with a child. Establish guidelines and enforce them, but listen to the child and be flexible based on respect, acceptance and wisdom, not on comfort or appeasement. You are meditating to help yourself, and therefore those who have to live with you, as well as the world in general. You can address whatever problems or issues that arise during your meditation at a later time.

If a thought, feeling or sound is a recurring interruption in your meditation, IDL strongly recommends that you address it outside your meditation in some practical way. Make a plan regarding how you are going to deal with it and handle it. If this does not stop it from interfering with your meditation, such as the noise from a building site across the street or someone practicing their Tuba upstairs, interview the noise, Tuba or some other related personification outside your meditation. You are thereby approaching it as if it were a "wake-up call" to which you need to listen. Doing so will generally move the distraction out of the role of Persecutor and into a more neutral space.

Don't attempt to focus on your distraction during meditation and imagine you are meditating, because you are either amplifying your distraction or focusing on repressing your distraction. The exception to this rule is if you completely merge with or identify with the sound of the Tuba, the noise from the building site, the pain in your back or some thought or feeling. If you can make such a move it is excellent because you both integrate the disruption into your sense of self while expanding it. However, this is typically a post-graduate level approach to distractions that few are able to manage, because we are typically too subjectively enmeshed in our thoughts, feelings and sensations to objectify them and then become one with them.

Instead, it is generally preferable to use IDL interviewing after meditation to listen to what the distraction has to say to you and then to take that identification into future meditations when and if it arises. Such interviews will more than likely disclose to you why the "distraction" comes up for you while providing you with a number of concrete recommendations for how to address it. IDL then recommends that you choose those recommendations that make sense to you, check them against external authorities and your common sense, and act on them.

See if such clear and focused helping does not change your relationship to the "distraction" during future meditations. Perhaps the pain does not go away when you meditate, but you now have re-framed it in such a way that it no longer is experienced as persecuting, but instead actually becomes a stimulus to deepen and broaden your sense of clarity and equanimity. While this may sound impossible and idealistic, IDL asks you to suspend your disbelief, conduct your own experiments, and draw your own conclusions.

The third way that a Rescuer is different from a helper is that a rescuer doesn't stop "helping" when the job is done. Instead, they keep on keeping on, out of a desire to validate their own self-worth, disguised as love, compassion and infinite

21: Meditation and the Drama Triangle

self-sacrifice. This shows up in meditation as a determination not to listen to yourself, but instead to continue to use tools and approaches that you have either outgrown or that no longer work for you. Perhaps you use them because some guru told you that is the way to meditate or because you can't imagine any other approach. In any case, the result of using meditation tools as forms of self-rescuing is that you may have little success meditating yet trudge on, out of a sense of dedication, self-sacrifice, and because you "should," despite your lack of success and your inability to expand or deepen your awareness when you meditate. Such a lack of improvement are signs for you to ask yourself, "Instead of listening to what I need when I meditate, am I forcing my own agenda or that of some spiritual teacher onto my practice?"

IDL uses naming during meditation to objectify whatever role in the Drama Triangle you are in at the moment. It is based on the principle that you cannot change what you are not aware of and that therefore when you name something you not only call it into your awareness but you focus your awareness on it instead of on an infinite number of other possibilities. For example, imagine you are distracted during your meditation by the sound of the fan or ventilation system. You think, "I am aware of the sound of the ventilation system," or "ventilation system," or "sound." You are simply naming what is in your awareness without putting a value on it: "BAD sound!" "Distracting sound!" You then name whatever next arises in your awareness; "I am aware of wondering what time it is." Then you name what comes up next: "I am aware I am not meditating but thinking about these distractions!" Then you name what comes up next: "I am aware I am irritated at myself and getting frustrated!" Continue naming. By doing so you do several things. You do not place positive or negative value on objects of your awareness. You are not saying, "This awareness is good (a Rescuer) and this one is bad (a Persecutor.) Instead, you are simply naming each as it arises. Secondly, you are interrupting your normal train of thought which serves to keep you trapped in the Drama Triangle. Normally, one thought leads to the next and to the next in habitual chains of self-rescuing validation. These chains are highly addictive, as you will discover when you realize that you have stopped naming and gotten lost in one of them. When you attempt to start naming again you may experience resistance, which indicates that floating down river, carried by first this, then that current of thought, is self-rescuing and the act of naming itself has magically taken on the role of Persecutor! What to do? You have three choices. You can name that as well, you can shift to some type of breath awareness, or you can stop meditating, refocus, and return later to meditation. You don't have to sit there and tough it out. That will easily put you into the role of Victim. You will find more on naming in *Waking Up*.

Your breathing can be used as a second, very sophisticated tool, to move you out of the Drama Triangle. *Seven Octaves of Enlightenment: Integral Deep*

21: Meditation and the Drama Triangle

Listening Pranayama is an in-depth guide for doing so. By observing each of six stages of every breath you shift your attention from your thoughts, feelings and images to a grounding, centering sensory awareness, thereby turning your breath into a Helper instead of an always present irrelevancy, like your shadow. This practice associates thoughts, values and feelings with different stages of each breath depending on the octave you are dealing with at the time. This can be thought of as a naming practice used in conjunction with observation of breath, further strengthening objectivity and detachment from other thoughts, feelings, images and sensations. Observation of breathing itself is another ladder which, when climbed, if not abandoned, becomes another form of self-rescue.

A third powerful tool IDL uses to wake up out of the Drama Triangle in meditation is similar to Tibetan Deity Yoga. It involves identification with interviewed emerging potentials that score high in qualities that are conducive to good meditation. For example, if you interview a hedgehog that scores ten in witnessing and you want to develop your ability to observe the contents of your awareness, including your tendency to fall into drama, you could do worse than to "become" this hedgehog while you are meditating and let it meditate for you.

Why would this be more effective than becoming an obviously sacred avatar, such as Manjusri or Avalokiteshvara? There are several reasons. These Tibetan Bodhisattvas are sacred for Tibetan Buddhists but are they for you? Because Amun Ra, Quetzalocoatl or Odin were sacred within their respective cultures, could you expect to get equivalent results from using them? The advantage of your hedgehog is that he is intrinsic to your consciousness in various ways and that his ability to witness is anchored to your current level of development, meaning that he is more likely to provide a type of witnessing that will work for you. In addition, while you may very well work with some emerging potential that is obviously sacred, like Jesus, working with those which are not, such as a hedgehog, expands your definition of what it means for something or someone to be sacred. You thereby move beyond appearances of sacred and secular as well as cultural assumptions about what is meaningful and what is not, to your own personal relationship with the perspective the hedgehog embodies. After all, can any one give you any intrinsic reason why Mother Mary or Buddha have to be more sacred or meaningful for you than nail clippers or a pile of dog shit?

Becoming, for example, a pile of dog shit that scores high in some quality you want to develop, such as inner peace, works because dog shit is completely unhinged from social and cultural definitions of what sacred sources of inner peace are supposed to look like. What this does in turn is add a potent element of cosmic humor to your meditation, meaning you add a certain lightness, not taking yourself or your practice so seriously that you crush the life out of it.

This points to another important point, that ongoing interviews will provide you with new, fresh and appropriate perspectives to take with you into meditation that

21: Meditation and the Drama Triangle

will work to balance and thereby move your practice forward into a state of flow.

One challenge that routinely comes up in identifying with this or that previously interviewed perspective, like our hedgehog or pile of dog shit, is that it is difficult to stay identified with any perspective that is different from our own. It is natural to drift out of "hedgehog consciousness" and back into our own, generally without realizing it. This is avoided during IDL interviewing by the asking of numerous questions that require role identification to answer. However, this option is not available during meditation because meditation is not a time for asking such questions, although as we shall see there are some types that may be useful.

The Tibetans deal with this issue by having meditators first contemplate a picture or statue of the deity to internalize and then to contemplate its image, in exquisite detail, mentally. However, contemplating an image is not the same as identifying with it. While it is true that our attention stays focused on the various attributes of the image, that is something less than taking on the persona of the image and looking at life from its perspective during meditation or normal waking life. To deal with this issue, IDL recommends that you ask repeatedly, during your meditation, whenever you become aware that you have lost touch with your hedgehog or pile of dog shit, "As this hedgehog, what am I thinking/feeling/doing/experiencing at this moment?" To take this question seriously requires empathy and identification on your part, meaning that you will shift back into its perspective during your meditation, a perspective which is much less immersed in the Drama Triangle than you are.

All of these understandings about the relationship between the Drama Triangle and meditation, as well as the tools of naming, observation of breath and identification with emerging potentials can only be proven with regular practice. Meditation is a yoga, a discipline. If you take it seriously and make it a priority in your daily routine it will speed your evolution out of the Drama Triangle, particularly if you experiment with these tools.

22: Lucid Dreaming and the Drama Triangle

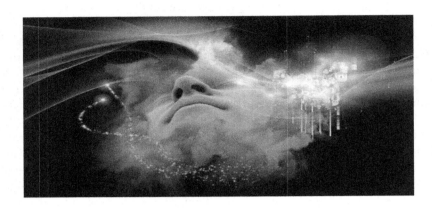

Lucid dreaming is generally thought of as waking up while you are dreaming with the object of experiencing greater freedom, choice, possibilities for confronting fears, learning new skills, having new experiences such as fantastic sex, traveling to other worlds or dimensions or learning from exalted teachers. IDL expands on this definition by viewing lucidity as any process of awakening, whether awake or asleep and dreaming, with the recognition that other forms of dream awakening exist that are as important or more important than lucid dreaming, or realizing that you are dreaming while you are in a dream.

One of these forms of lucidity that is extremely important is waking up out of the Drama Triangle in whatever state of consciousness you are in. Based on years of observing the transformations of dream content of those who have worked with IDL, recognizing and neutralizing the Drama Triangle in your relationships and thinking will definitely reduce its prominence in your dreams. This is a vital form of lucidity, because lucid dreaming itself provides no guarantee that you are out of the Drama Triangle. Indeed, if you do not know how to escape it in your relationships and thoughts, it is highly likely to be carried into your dreams. There are many examples of lucid dreams that include the Drama Triangle.

When you become lucid in dreams and change or manipulate the dream, instead of waking up by listening to and learning from the dream drama, you are probably unknowingly exporting your waking biases and misperceptions into the dreamscape, conquering it and manipulating it. This is a basic problem with most approaches to lucid dreaming – they underestimate how our perceptual context frames, affects and limits lucid dream experience. With lucid dreaming we infuse the dream with greater self-awareness, which is valuable, particularly if our self-awareness is evolved enough to *listen* rather than merely *control*. However, this is generally not the case. For most of us, the self that wakes up in a dream is itself sleepwalking through life. That "awake" self is itself developmentally arrested. It's like putting a drunk behind the steering wheel of a car.

We might consider such a situation as self-persecution within the Drama Triangle in the context of lucid dreaming. You become lucid in a dream and change it according to your wishes without considering the interests of the other characters in the dream. To understand how this is abuse, switch roles. How do you feel when people come into your life and demand that you change to meet their expectations? Your dream lucidity ideally supports the agenda of your life compass instead of simply colonizing your dream world with your own waking agenda. However, to learn to recognize and follow the priorities of your life compass requires some methodology that differentiates them from your conscience, religious and spiritual scripting and the recommendations of teachers and gurus. This is a major objective of IDL interviewing of dream characters and the personifications of your life issues.

Lucidity will be both reinforced and speeded up in all three realms, waking relationships, thinking and dreaming, if you also take steps to reduce the Drama Triangle in your dreams. This is a form of lucid dreaming that is different from realizing while you are dreaming that you are asleep and dreaming; it is a lucidity that involves recognizing invitations into the Drama Triangle while you are dreaming and saying "no thanks." Waking up to the presence of the Drama Triangle becomes more likely when pre-sleep suggestion is used, but more importantly, when IDL is used to interview dream Persecutors, Rescuers and Victims. This is because the Drama Triangle is thereby objectified in a way that not only reduces its frequency and intensity while dreaming, but in the other two realms of relationships and thinking. Alex shared the following dream in which he went lucid:

"I am in a jail. I have to take care of people on death row. I'm not a prisoner but I'm not a caretaker. I'm something in-between. I am taking care of people in the last hours before they go to the electric chair. One of them is a former male friend. He knows that he will die in a few hours. I have to cheer him up. It's not a good time for me. (Crying). It's dark with all the fear of losing him. I have to tell him that I love him and that he's a good guy. I have to cheer him up for his last hours. It's awful. Then they take him out of the room and take him to kill him. I have to stay there until they bring him back dead. I try to wake up because I realize it's a nightmare, but I can't stop dreaming. I knew I was dreaming but I couldn't wake up; I couldn't stop it. The next person is my grandmother. I have to take care of her. They take her and kill her and I have to wait for the body to come back on a stretcher. Then I woke up, went back to sleep and the same thing was happening to other people. Even with waking up I couldn't stop this nightmare."

22: Lucid Dreaming and the Drama Triangle

Alex could see that the grip of this "dream" was so powerful that, as with a post-traumatic stress nightmare, he could not "awaken" from it, even after he was fully awake. Alex recognized that his attempts to wake up out of his nightmare were self-rescuing attempts at avoidance, within the context of the Drama Triangle.

Alex knew, as soon as he woke up, that these people who were getting murdered were parts of himself. He recognized that he was remorseful about the death of parts of himself and that in his dream he was responsible for their murders. He could also see that his unsuccessful attempts at going lucid within the dream or in awakening from it were attempts at self-rescuing.

Most of us have had similar experiences at one time or another; we want to wake up, we fight to wake up, but we can't. What's going on? On one level, this is a mirroring of our waking experience; we are caught in some self-rescuing addiction and cannot escape. It may be chronic worrying, an explosive temper, pornography, eating, a drug addiction, wasting our time surfing the internet, or self-criticism. Whatever it is, if we try to break it, to escape from it, the experience is very much an attempt to arouse ourselves out of a dreamlike repetitive life pattern and failing to do so.

What would going lucid accomplish for this dreamer? Would it create insight into his fear or self-abuse or simply a change the dream to a more comfortable theme, subject or context? Would it result in enlightenment or mere relief? Wouldn't it be counter-productive, because it would merely serve to avoid, repress, and deny the nightmare? In such lucidity, in such "enlightenment," there is little freedom, control, autonomy or ability to change that which created, and it may well in the future re-create a nightmare that embraces everyday consciousness.

Clearly, Alex's nightmare is demanding that it be *heard*, not ignored, repressed, or changed into something else. Going lucid in the nightmare is a failed attempt by Alex to rescue himself from the Drama Triangle roles of self-persecution, self-victimization, and self-rescuing by waking up. The "reality" of the nightmare is experienced as a source of persecution; Alex experiences himself as the Victim of that persecution. He seeks rescuing through lucidity, changing the dream, or waking up.

The nature of the Drama Triangle is such that if you play one role, you eventually play them all. Therefore, by rescuing himself from the nightmare in some fashion Alex becomes his own persecutor; his nightmares are only likely to become louder and ever more pervasive. "Self-rescuing" is not the same thing as helping yourself. It is more akin to addiction, in which you do something that feels good or relieves your stress but which keeps you struck in self-persecution, self-abuse, and self-victimization.

This is an excellent example of why lucidity, waking up, freedom, and enlightenment are not ends in themselves. For example, in traditional Hindu and Buddhist metaphysics, the world is *maya,* a delusional realm of ignorance and suffering, from which one seeks freedom as *samadhi* in Hinduism and *nirvana* in Buddhism. No one ever stops to think that this puts earthly existence in the role of Persecutor, oneself in the role of Victim, simply by the fact that you are alive, and freedom in the role of Rescuer. This is not merely a critique of Buddhism and Hinduism, or even of all religions, but of all forms of self-rescuing.

Many people associate lucid dreaming with spirituality, when in fact children and criminals can lucid dream. Is lucid dreaming about higher levels of personal development? Is there any correlation between someone's ability to lucid dream and their empathy, altruism, or compassion? While there are many legitimate reasons to lucid dream, as we have seen, you are wise to learn to ask, both awake and dreaming, "Is what I am doing, or wanting to do, a form of self-rescuing within the Drama Triangle?" If you look at your life in this context it is not difficult to find self-rescuing aspects in everything you do: the foods you choose to eat and not eat, who you spend time with, when and why you answer and write emails or use the internet, why you go to work, why you pay your bills, why you meditate and do other spiritual practices, and why you exercise. Again, there is nothing intrinsically wrong with any of these activities; *it is only when they are done within the Drama Triangle* that they create misery and suffering in your life. If you attempt to wake up out of them by self-rescuing, you put yourself in a position similar to that of Alex in his nightmare.

Are there any activities undertaken in pursuit of enlightenment, including lucid dreaming, that are never attempts at self-rescue? Of course there are, but the assumption of self-rescue is a reasonable and wise default position. Are there any situations in which self-rescue can be done without keeping you stuck in the Drama Triangle? Yes, when you "wake up," when are you not contaminating a wider realm, whether it be dream sleep, dreamless sleep, near death, or mystical experience with the delusional assumptions inherent in your waking worldview. Why and how is it reasonable to assume that you become free or liberated from your own assumptions and perceptual prison simply because you have shifted to an awareness that you are asleep and dreaming? Are we not still asleep, dreaming, sleepwalking, and delusional within our particular perceptual framework? An example in waking life is the aliveness and relative wakefulness we experience when we fall in love, go on vacation, move into a new home, job or city, or have expanded, transformative realizations from a teaching or guru. As time passes, we find that we have two challenges: to stay awake and to integrate our new degree of wakefulness into the routines of our everyday life. Most of us find that just as with lucid dreaming, we fall back into states of habitual sleepwalking.

This is often very difficult to identify because the experience of freedom, expansiveness, unconditional love, and timelessness are so overwhelming that we feel transformed. But are we? Is there anything inherently transformative about moving into a relatively unconditioned context? If you go to the Mediterranean for a vacation the freedom from your normal routines combined with a host of new sights, sounds, and places is experienced as liberating. Is it? Well, yes and no. Most people, most of the time, quickly discover one of two things. Either they cannot integrate the "otherness" of the Mediterranean into their everyday life and so either forget about it or live a split life, always missing it and longing for it, or they import all their bad habits into their new life on the Mediterranean. They continue to smoke, drink, worry, nag, or whatever, in short, continue their lives within the tender embrace of the Drama Triangle.

Ken Wilber discusses this in terms of the grandiosity of an amplified sense of self, which can appear in advanced meditators experiencing oneness with nature, deity, or formlessness.[13] IDL honors the nightmares of your life by giving them the respect that follows from suspending judgments, listening, and applying what makes sense. Instead of changing the nightmare or dream, whether awake or dreaming, to conform to your assumptions of happiness, you experience multi-perspectival contexts that transcend and include your own.

There are many legitimate uses for dream lucidity, such as using them to develop confidence in dealing with fears, in practicing life skills in the fail-safe circumstance of a death-free dream reality, and in creating healing possibilities that do not exist in waking life. All of these are good; still more important is to learn to interview other characters in your dreams while you are dreaming in order to benefit from their perspective. Even more important than lucid dreaming is to learn to meditate in your dreams.

Self-rescuing needs to be compared to its healthy alternative, helping. When you help yourself you are not reacting to your compulsive behaviors and addictions out of a desire to escape from them. Instead, you develop a plan, check with sources of objectivity to see if it is realistic, engage whatever support systems are necessary for it to succeed, monitor your progress, and check again with those sources of objectivity to see if your progress is genuine or whether you are fooling yourself, such as by replacing one addiction with another. You begin this process of helping yourself in your dreams and nightmares, not necessarily by attempting to go lucid, but by asking questions: "Who are you?" "Are you a part of me? If so, what parts of me do you most closely represent?" "Are you attempting to scare me?" "If so, why?"

If you remembered to ask such questions of your experience, lucid or not, what do you think would be the most likely result? Wouldn't you wake up in your awareness, in your consciousness, *within the dream or nightmare?* Isn't this what life is wanting to do in and through us? If the object of life was to escape, why be

---

13 Wilber, K. *Transformations of Consciousness.* New Science Library, 1986.

22: Lucid Dreaming and the Drama Triangle

alive in the first place? Why not just die? We are here to wake up, not just to ourselves or to life, but to life's priorities and agenda. The more that we then thin ourselves and get out of the way, the more life takes on the sacred experience of oneness with life itself. While it is possible to attempt to become lucid while dreaming, our destiny is to learn how to be lucid in all states. As you wake up out of the Drama Triangle today, now in your relationships and thoughts you will find that transformational clarity reflected in your dreams, lucid and otherwise.

23: Near Death Experiences and the Drama Triangle

Near Death Experiences are normally described as timeless, spaceless, transformational experiences of oneness with deep love and acceptance. They are so objectively "other" than normal, everyday experience that there is certainty that they are real, true and universal, that is, real not only for the beholder, but for anyone at any time or place, because they are experiences of the reality behind life itself.

As the skunk at the picnic, IDL agrees with integral that truth is contextual, that is, that any reality, which integral calls a "holon," that is objectively real, will at some point be found to be conditioned by wider, more inclusive holons that contain and transcend it. The conclusion to be drawn is that just because an experience is infinite, timeless, blissful and all-encompassing in its compassion for us is no reason to believe it will always be that way or that it will be that way for all others, regardless of our own certainty.

A mundane example of this phenomena is falling head over heels in love. We are sure it is right and the other person is our "soul mate." It is only later, when we have broadened our context, that we are able to contextualize or relativize our experience and begin to understand why our friends and family did not share the same enthusiasm. Often we end up telling ourselves, "What was I thinking"

Many people want to claim that NDEs are so transcendent and transformational that this concept of contexts does not apply. However, the evidence that they give is experiential, at its base no different from the evidence young lovers give for their delirium. In addition, if we read over accounts of near death experiences it is not unusual to find instances of the Drama Triangle. When we step back and view near death experiences in the context of the life of the experiencer, we find even more evidence of the Drama Triangle.

For example, here is a passage from a near death narrative: "I tried to see something, but all there was to see was this cyclonic void that tapered into a funnel. I kept grabbing at the sides but my fingers had nothing to grasp. Terror set in, true terror. I saw a black spot, darker than the funnel and like a black curtain, falling in front of me. Then there was a white dot, like a bright light at the end of the funnel. But as I grew closer, it was a small white skull. It became larger, grinning at me with bare sockets and gaping mouth, and traveling straight toward me like a baseball. Not only was I terrified, I was really livid, too. I struggled to grab hold of anything to keep me from falling, but the skull loomed larger. 'My kids, my baby is so little. My little boy, he's only two years old. No!' My words rang in my head and ears. With a bellowing yell, I screamed: 'No! damn it, no! Let me go. My babies need me! No! No! No! No!'"[14]

Here we have a skull as Persecutor, the experiencer as Victim, and self-rescuing attempts at bargaining. However, IDL does not view drama as intrinsic to life or to near death experiences, but rather an artifact of human perception and conditioning. Because people are not aware of the Drama Triangle and how they are immersed in it they are likely to project it onto whatever they experience in whatever realm they are in at the time. This is obvious with waking and dreaming, but not so obvious with mystical and near death experiences.

Some percentage of near death experiencers are "homesick," meaning that they are no longer comfortable in the world. Overwhelmed by the beauty, freedom, magnificence, peace and love of their near death experience, they do not want to return to normal life. When they do, it feels like a prison, a term in jail to which they have been sentenced. Longing to be free, to return to paradise, they may live in near suicidal depression. The reality of their NDE is their Rescuer and life in the world is now their Persecutor. Because they cannot escape from this nightmarish bad dream, they are a Victim. Life, death and paradise now all exist within the Drama Triangle.

What are we to make of the many NDEs that contain Rescuers in the form of deceased loved ones, angels and beckoning glorious lights at the end of dark tunnels? What are we to make of the accounts of Persecuting entities or experiences that occur in some NDEs? A mainstream interpretation is to say, "The good stuff is real while the bad stuff is a projection of one's own shadow." Integral theory calls this "elevationism," one example of the pre-trans fallacy. We are made powerless through the externalization of the good because it so transcends all definitions we have of who we are and we are also thrown into conflict with ourselves by defining the bad stuff as self-generated.

IDL holds that the depth of our conviction that an NDE is ultimately and

---

14 Atwater, P.M.H., *Beyond the Light,* Birch Lane Press, NYC, 1995.

externally real is a reflection of the depth of our disownership of important innate potentials, just as the presence of the Drama Triangle within an NDE is a statement of its presence as a pervasive perceptual cognitive distortion in which we are subjectively enmeshed. These are reasons why the book, *"Fire From Heaven: Deep Listening to Near Death Experiences"* was written.[15]

---

15 Dillard, J. *Fire From Heaven: Deep Listening to Near Death Experiences*, Deep Listening Press, Berlin, 2013. https://www.createspace.com/4196946

Alphabetical Index

addiction.....**2, 4, 17, 27, 32p., 36, 45p., 51p., 54, 68, 109, 125, 128, 143p., 154, 164, 166**
Advaita Vedanta..21
agape...45p.
alcohol..3, 48p., 51, 63
Amun Ra..160
annata..22
anxiety..5p., 21, 37, 51, 99, 124pp., 137, 152
Apollo..1
AQAL..23, 112p.
Atman...21p., 95, 114
Avalokiteshvara..160
avidya...21, 152, 154
Beck..25
Big Oil...150
bioresonance..9, 109
blame...3pp., 15, 37, 56, 72pp., 76, 101, 153
Blankfein...12
Bodhisattva..57, 160
Brahman..21p., 95
Buddha..1, 21, 97, 152, 160
Buddhist...21, 90, 97, 155, 160, 165
burn-out...9, 14, 26, 81, 153
Burns..25
chakra...48, 116
Clear Light...21
cognitive distortion...**6, 13, 25, 28pp., 37, 40, 59p., 73, 78, 82, 89, 94, 114, 119, 136, 144, 155, 170**
Collapse..92, 146
conscience..40, 74p., 79pp., 96, 101, 103, 108
Deep Listening.....................................4, 17, 21, 119, 130, 152, 159
defense mechanisms..38
depression..5p., 9, 24, 37, 51, 126p., 169
dharma...22, 47, 96
Diamond..92, 146

Dream Sociometry...**144**
dukkha..**21, 23, 28p., 53, 97, 116, 133, 152**
Eckhart...**155**
emerging potentials......**30, 33, 41pp., 61, 81p., 89pp., 97, 114p., 117, 120, 138, 156, 160**
Enlightenment...**4**
eros...**45p., 60**
escapism..**3, 17, 63**
Fire From Heaven...**170**
Frederic Laloux,..**147**
George Bush..**12**
God. **3, 12, 21p., 43p., 47, 74, 79, 81pp., 85p., 91, 93, 95, 99pp., 108, 116, 153, 155**
Goldman Sachs..**12**
Gotama..**21**
guilt......................................**2pp., 37, 74, 80, 82pp., 87, 101, 103p., 141**
guru...**9, 94p., 115**
Guru..**47, 49p.**
Hindu..**21p., 54, 90, 95pp., 103, 105, 109, 154p., 165**
holon..**23, 25, 151, 168**
IDL..**166**
Inquisition..**1**
integral....................................**16, 23, 26, 110pp., 119, 133, 135, 144, 168**
Integral Deep Listening Interviewing Techniques...**4**
integral life practice...**114, 133, 135**
internal individual quadrant..**25**
interpersonal..**2, 8, 23p., 100, 112p., 152**
Islam..**1, 103pp., 148**
Israel...**7, 101, 103p., 148**
Jesus...**1, 93, 102pp., 160**
Judaism..**7, 100pp.**
Julius Caesar..**1**
karma..........**7, 21p., 47p., 53, 90p., 93, 95pp., 103, 109, 116, 137, 152, 155**
Karpman..**1**
life compass...........**5, 32, 39, 42, 80pp., 84, 87p., 91p., 94, 96p., 108p., 163**
Lincoln...**1**
loneliness..**10, 46pp.**

Lord of the Rings......19, 62
Lovelock......151
lucid......5, 21, 26, 42, 55p., 117, 122, 141, 162pp.
lucid dreaming......5, 21, 42, 55, 117, 162p., 165p.
Manjusri......160
matrix......4
maya......21p., 53, 152, 165
Meditation......4
metaphysical......22p., 26, 44, 47, 86, 89, 94, 96
monotheism......21, 105
must......3p., 21, 35, 75pp., 80, 82p., 87, 101, 103, 112, 122, 138
nightmare......2, 16, 20, 29, 37, 39p., 125p., 128, 143, 163pp.
Oberon......9, 109
Odin......160
Oedipus Rex......19
Othello......19
ought......4, 75p., 80
Padmasambhava......21
Patanjali......155
perceptual cognitive distortion....13, 28pp., 89, 94, 114, 119, 136, 155, 170
personalization......12p., 46, 144
philos......46, 66, 112
Plato......146
poverty......10, 145
Prana......4
Pride and Prejudice......19
PTSD......20
Quetzalocoatl......160
reincarnation......21p., 123
Reinventing Organizations......147
Republican Party......150
Rifkin......151
samsara......21, 97, 116, 154
self-persecution......2, 4pp., 54, 76, 120, 164
Seven Octaves of Enlightenment: Integral Deep Listening Pranayama...159
Shankara......21
should **4pp., 11, 22, 36, 40p., 68, 74pp., 80, 84, 87p., 103, 119, 132p., 136,**

141, 159
sin....**1, 4, 7, 10pp., 16pp., 21pp., 26, 33p., 36, 38pp., 47p., 51, 54, 59pp., 63, 68pp., 72pp., 81p., 85p., 89pp., 99pp., 107, 109, 113, 116, 118pp., 122p., 125, 127, 129, 131pp., 136p., 139, 144, 151pp., 155pp., 163, 166, 168**
Socrates...46
Socratic Triune...23, 58, 89p.
soul mate..16, 40, 48
St. Augustine...22
St. John of the Cross 155
stress..............**9, 21, 51, 65, 75, 121p., 124pp., 128, 130, 137, 139, 154, 164**
suffering **6, 17, 21pp., 26, 28pp., 53, 55, 68, 72, 96p., 108, 116, 132p., 152, 155, 165**
tantra...51
Ten Commandments...74, 89
Tertullian...22
Tibetan Deity Yoga...160
Tolkein...19, 62
Transactional Analysis...23p., 141, 152
Waking Up..4
Wilber..23, 112, 114p., 123, 166
Yoga...4
Zionism..7

Made in the USA
Las Vegas, NV
20 August 2022